VGM Opportunities Serie

D0167251

OPPORTUNITIES IN **OCCUPATIONAL THERAPY CAREERS**

Marguerite Abbott
Marie-Louise Franciscus
Zona R. Weeks

Foreword by
Mary Evert
Former President
The American Occupational Therapy Association, Inc.

Revised by
Marguerite Duffy

VGM Career Books
NTC/Contemporary Publishing Group

Library of Congress Cataloging-in-Publication Data

Abbot, Marguerite.
    Opportunities in occupational therapy careers / Marguerite Abbott, Marie-Louise
Franciscus, Zona R. Weeks ; foreword by Mary Evert.—Rev. ed.
        p. cm. — (VGM opportunities series)
      ISBN 0-658-00472-7 (cloth) — ISBN 0-658-00473-5 (paper)
    1. Occupational therapy—Vocational guidance. I. Franciscus, Marie
Louise. II. Weeks, Zona Roberta, 1936– III. Title. IV. Series.

RM735.4 .A22 2000
615.8'515'023—dc21

                                                                        00-31995

Published by VGM Career Books
A division of NTC/Contemporary Publishing Group, Inc.
4255 West Touhy Avenue, Lincolnwood (Chicago), Illinois 60712-1975 U.S.A.
Printed in the United States of America.
International Standard Book Number: 0-658-00472-7 (cloth)
                                     0-658-00473-5 (paper)

 01   02   03   04   LB   16   15   14   13   12   11   10   9   8   7   6   5   4   3   2   1

DEDICATION

This volume is dedicated to
the occupational therapy students of the
world—those who are, those who have
been, and those who will be.

CONTENTS

ABOUT THE AUTHORS

Following graduation from the Grier School in Tyrone, Pennsylvania, Marie-Louise Franciscus received a diploma from the Philadelphia School of Occupational Therapy, a Bachelor of Science degree from Ohio State University, a Master of Arts degree in special education, and a certificate in student personnel administration from Teachers College of Columbia University. Additionally, the author completed postgraduate instruction in many areas of specialization through workshops and institutes: cerebral palsy, therapeutic exercise, psychiatry, curriculum planning, administration, group process, graduate education, and the creative process.

In the clinical field, Professor Franciscus has worked with patients in a hospital for the mentally ill, a residential school for children with cerebral palsy, a hospital for children with orthopedic and cardiac conditions, and a general hospital of the U.S. Army.

As an administrator, the author has guided the development of several occupational therapy treatment services. She served for many years as an educational administrator, concerned with curriculum planning and development. Her last position was that of Professor and Director of Occupational Therapy Programs, College of Physicians and Surgeons, Columbia University.

Marguerite Abbott received her professional diploma from the Boston School of Occupational Therapy, Boston, Massachusetts, and a Bachelor of Science degree from Tufts University. She received her Master of Arts degree and professional certificate in university administration from Columbia University. She completed a postgraduate course in the treatment of cerebral palsy at the Children's Rehabilitation Institute, under the direction of Dr. Winthrop Phelps. She was also a teaching fellow in human dissection at the School of Occupational Therapy, College of Physicians and Surgeons, Columbia University.

Professor Abbott was a member of the faculty of medicine, Occupational Therapy, at Columbia for many years in the capacity of director, administrator, writer, and teacher. On the 25th anniversary of Columbia's Occupational Therapy School, the alumni awarded a Certificate of Recognition to her for her creative administration, teaching, and outstanding leadership in the clinical and educational fields. She had more than forty publications, some of which have worldwide coverage in three languages. She was a recognized authority, nationally and internationally, in professional education.

Her clinical experience included many years of directorships in the fields of pediatrics, administration, and physical dysfunction, together with clinical and university teaching.

Internationally, she was a member of the World Federation of Occupational Therapists and served on the Expert Advisory Committee of that organization. She spent many years as a consultant-teacher abroad and organized graduate courses for teaching at the Aistley-Ainsley Rehabilitation Hospital, Edinburgh, Scotland. She was a well-known lecturer, both here and abroad, in occupational therapy education and cerebral palsy.

Zona Weeks received her Bachelor of Science Degree in occupational therapy from the University of Wisconsin, a Master of Science degree in educational psychology from Butler University, and a Doctor of Philosophy degree in educational psychology from Indiana University. Her clinical experience has been in occupational therapy for physical dysfunction, with primary emphasis on sensorimotor integration as a basis for treatment. She is also a licensed school psychologist, allowing her to combine experience with learning disabilities and occupational therapy evaluations to more fully understand difficulties related to learning, social-emotional functioning, and movement disorders.

Dr. Weeks served as a faculty member in occupational therapy at the Indiana University School of Medicine before leaving to establish and become the founding director of two occupational therapy Master of Science degree programs at the University of Indianapolis: a professional entry-level master's degree program and a postprofessional master's degree program.

Professionally, Dr. Weeks has been active at state and national levels. She has served as President of the Indiana Occupational Therapy Association, and President of the Indiana Allied Health Association. Nationally, in addition to serving on several committees, she has been a Regional Research Consultant for the American Occupational Therapy Foundation, on whose executive board she served, and she has held positions on the editorial review boards of *The American Journal of Occupational Therapy* and *The Occupational Therapy Journal of Research.* She is currently on the editorial review board of *Cognitive Rehabilitation.* She has published several book chapters and journal articles. Dr. Weeks has been honored by being named a Fellow of the American Occupational Therapy Association.

This edition has been thoroughly revised and updated by Marguerite Duffy.

FOREWORD

Over the past decade, the demand for occupational therapy services has skyrocketed along with employment opportunities, salaries, and benefits. Some of this growth has come about as nearly every country in the world attempts to include individuals with disabilities in the workplace and the community. Practitioners in this field make valuable contributions to society in any number of ways. Occupational therapists and occupational therapy assistants are helping employers and business owners to make their premises more accessible and less likely to cause injury or disability. They also aid employers, employees, and those with disabilities in workplace integration for people with disabilities.

In America, occupational therapy services are a critical component of efforts to assist the growing number of people dealing with problems related to aging, and for infants and children with problems associated with prematurity or birth defects. The many individuals surviving accidents and illness with significant difficulties in meeting their daily needs benefit from interventions offered by occupational therapy personnel.

Occupational therapy is based on the use of everyday activities as the means of helping people to achieve independence.

Certified occupational therapy personnel consist of occupational therapists and occupational therapy assistants. The occupational therapy assistant completes a two year associate degree program while the occupational therapist enters the field with a bachelor's degree or master's degree. Opportunities for advancement are many and varied as are the types of disabling conditions, the ages of individuals to receive services, and the settings in which one might work. Many seek graduate education, opting to shift into roles of educator, researcher, consultant, administrator, or master clinician.

Employment and private enterprise opportunities in the field of occupational therapy are expanding and diversifying. Community and home-based programs offer personnel options to deliver direct primary health care, to conduct research, and to manage programs offering services to people with a wide variety of physical, emotional, and educational disabling conditions. Many more occupational therapists and occupational therapy assistants are needed in school systems. Those with an entrepreneurial spirit find private practice attractive.

Practitioners also enjoy the freedom to move from one work setting to another in order to meet changing personal and professional goals throughout their careers. Occupational therapists often manage treatment programs administered by a variety of individuals with differing educational preparation and professional credentials.

Occupational therapy's important role in our health care system is likely to significantly expand as a result of reforms being developed in the United States. Working directly with clients in the home, community, school, and workplace using everyday activities people want and need to perform, occupational therapy practitioners improve the prospects of a satisfying, productive life for millions of Americans.

Mary M. Evert, MBA, OTR, FAOTA
Former President, The American Occupational
Therapy Association

PREFACE

According to the United States Department of Labor, occupational therapy is one of the fastest growing health professions in the nation. In recent years the profession has undergone tremendous change and development, stimulated both from within and from societal pressures to fill specific health care needs. At the initiative of practitioners, there has been an elaboration and clarification of the profession's underlying philosophies, frames of reference, and knowledge bases. Technological advances and increased knowledge, with development of new theoretical rationales and techniques for treatment, have resulted in increasingly effective health care delivery. Occupational therapy has expanded to meet society's demands for health care service in new areas for which occupational therapists have the necessary expertise. This expertise is acquired during educational preparation involving extensive academic work and supervised clinical experiences.

Contributions of occupational therapists to health care delivery occur in the medical system (in hospitals or similar facilities) and in the community through various health-related agencies or health promotion programs. The primary concern is to restore an individual to a functional state for return to society, if possible. In the community and in the educational system in particular, the emphasis is on normal development and promotion of optimum health and life functioning.

There is an air of excitement in the profession of occupational therapy today, as clinicians, administrators, educators, and students reach for new professional horizons. This small book can only touch upon some of the many aspects of occupational therapy that might interest future students. It is hoped that this book may provide guidance and direction that will encourage the motivated reader to seek more detailed information and follow through with career education plans.

This edition has been revised to reflect some of the newer developments in the profession and to incorporate current educational program listings, salary levels, and other data.

Marie-Louise Franciscus, OTR
Zona R. Weeks, Ph.D., OTR, FAOTA

ACKNOWLEDGMENTS

We appreciate the assistance of staff members at The American Occupational Therapy Association, who provided necessary data used in this edition.

CHAPTER 1

AN OVERVIEW OF THE PROFESSION

Occupational therapy is a health care profession with a focus on "occupation." "Occupation" has more than one meaning, however. It may refer to life occupations or roles, including not only work roles but also such roles in life as preschooler, student, parent, etc. "Occupation" also refers to the process of doing (or occupying), and in occupational therapy it may be defined as tasks or activities with specific goals or purposes.

Occupational therapists attempt to minimize handicaps resulting from physical, developmental, cognitive, emotional, and social problems, and to help individuals obtain maximum independence. Skills for self-care, school or work, play or leisure, and interpersonal and group interactions are necessary for a satisfying, productive life. Developing new or lost skills is important, as is maintaining functional levels as long as possible in a person whose condition is declining. Quality of life and concern for the total individual are of prime importance. Occupational therapists realize that in dealing with human beings one cannot separate mind from body. They often incorporate psychological knowledge and methods to help them understand and work with persons having physical disabilities, and they would not overlook physical components in working with mentally ill persons.

Personal traits necessary for working in this profession are maturity, intelligence, imagination, patience, and teaching ability.

1

The ability to solve problems is important. Occupational therapists work to help patients or clients improve their functional level and seek their active participation in setting goals whenever possible.

The definition of occupational therapy accepted by the American Occupational Therapy Association Representative Assembly in 1981 is as follows:

> Occupational therapy is the use of purposeful activity with individuals who are limited by physical injury or illness, psychosocial dysfunction, developmental or learning disabilities, poverty and cultural differences or the aging process, in order to maximize independence, prevent disability, and maintain health. The practice encompasses evaluation, treatment and consultation. Specific occupational therapy services include teaching daily living skills; developing perceptual motor skills and sensory integrative functioning; developing play skills and prevocational and leisure capacities; designing, fabricating or applying selected orthotic and prosthetic devices or selective adaptive equipment; using specifically designed crafts and exercises to enhance functional performance; administering and interpreting tests such as manual muscle testing and range of motion; and adapting environments for the handicapped. These services are provided individually, in groups, or through social systems.

As you read the succeeding chapters, many aspects of occupational therapy should become clear, but potential students would be well advised to visit hospitals, schools, and other facilities to observe various types of occupational therapy practice.

Two levels of practice exist in the occupational therapy profession, represented by the registered occupational therapist (OTR) and the certified occupational therapy assistant (COTA). Occupational therapists evaluate patients or clients, plan their programs, and supervise or provide treatment. Occupational therapy assistants work with the occupational therapists in the planning and carrying out of treatment. The majority of occupational therapists enter the profession with a bachelor's degree in occupational therapy, but some enter with postbaccalaureate certificates, and others through entry-level master's degree programs, a few of which accept students with either a bachelor's degree in another field or a specified number of undergraduate semester hours and appropriate prerequisites. Occupational therapy assistants complete either an associate degree program or one of a small number of twelve to fourteen-month certificate programs. Greater detail regarding educational requirements may be found in Chapter 4, and a list of educational programs at both levels may be found in Appendix C.

THE PATIENT OR CLIENT

The terms "patient" or "client" are used to refer to persons receiving occupational therapy services. "Patient" is used in the medical system and "client" is more commonly used in the community system. Who is the patient or client? He or she may be a skilled worker who, because of an accident, has lost the ability to work; a child with learning disabilities because of delayed development accompanied by sensory-integrative or perceptual problems; a homemaker confined to a wheelchair because of arthritis; a stroke victim who must learn to speak, dress, and feed herself or himself again; an emotionally troubled person who must acquire the confidence to reenter the working world; a birth-injured child with multiple problems involving speech, vision, and motor control; or an amputee who must learn to use a prosthesis. The list is endless, fascinating, and challenging.

The functions of occupational therapy in relation to patient care, as adopted by the World Federation of Occupational Therapists in 1962, are listed below. Changes have occurred with technological advances and the expansion of practice areas, but the functions listed here remain pertinent:

1. As specific treatment for psychiatric patients, to structure opportunities for the development of more satisfying relationships, to assist in releasing or sublimating emotional drives, and to aid as a diagnostic tool.
2. As specific treatment for restoration of physical function, to increase joint motion, muscle strength, and coordination.
3. To teach self-help activities of daily living, such as eating, dressing, writing, and the use of adapted equipment and prostheses.
4. To help the disabled homemaker readjust to home routines with advice and instruction as to the adaptation of household equipment and work simplification.
5. To develop work tolerance and maintenance of special skills as required by the patient's job.
6. To provide prevocational exploration, to determine the patient's physical and mental capacities, social adjustment, interests, work habits, skills, and potential employability.
7. As a supportive measure, to help the patient to accept and utilize constructively a prolonged period of hospitalization and convalescence.
8. To redirect recreational and avocational interests.

Occupational therapists are concerned with the components of performance needed to maintain self-care, work, and play or leisure activities. These components include:

- Motor functioning (range of motion, muscle strength, tone, functional use, gross and fine motor skills);
- Sensory integrative functioning (body integration, body scheme, posture, visual-spatial awareness, sensorimotor integration, reflex and sensory development);
- Cognitive functioning (verbal and written communication, concentration, problem solving, time management, conceptualization, integration of learning);

- Psychological functioning (emotional states and feelings, coping behaviors, defense mechanisms, self-identity, self-concept); and
- Social functioning (one-to-one or group interactions).

The client population served by occupational therapy is representative of the total life span from infancy through old age. Occupational therapy serves those whose abilities to cope with the tasks of daily living are impaired by environmental deprivation; developmental defect; physical, emotional, or social trauma; illness; or the life demands and changes reflected in the aging process.

These services are primarily located in rehabilitation facilities, acute or chronic care hospitals, nursing homes, community agencies, children's schools, treatment centers, developmental institutions, senior citizens' centers, private homes, and private practice facilities. Other locations are diverse and may include research centers, industry, psychiatric centers, juvenile detention centers or prisons, camps for handicapped individuals, federal and state health agencies, and so forth. Occupational therapists may choose to work exclusively with children or adolescents, with only adults, or with a combination of children and adults, depending upon the setting selected for employment.

The tasks necessary to productive life at each age level are the treatment tools of the therapist: the activities used by the child to learn and grow through play; the socialization activities of adolescence; the homemaking, child-rearing, work-related activities of the adult; and the self-help skills that serve the individual throughout life, such as eating, dressing, personal hygiene, and communications.

The occupational therapist works collaboratively with members of other health-related professions and is an integral member of the professional team, which, though members vary in relation to the problem to be solved, may include qualified physicians, nurses, physical therapists, speech pathologists, social workers, psychologists, rehabilitation counselors, therapeutic recreation specialists, teachers, chaplains, counselors, and others. Specialists involved as needed might be artificial limb makers (prosthetists) and brace makers (orthotists).

The patient or client and his or her family are important members of the decision-making process regarding the management of the problem. The occupational therapist in many instances serves as an advisor in assisting the patient-family constellation in making decisions and in carrying out home-prescribed routines, such as exercises, follow-up management, and self-care procedures.

Within the medical framework, the ultimate responsibility for the patient rests with the physician in charge. The physician seeks information from others on which to base decisions, but it is he or she who prescribes medication, surgery, and the rehabilitation therapies, of which occupational therapy is one. The referral of an individual to the occupational therapist requires that an evaluation be made of ability and loss of ability and that a performance treatment plan be formulated.

In a community setting a therapist may be functioning as an extension of a medical institution and will work under the above referral system. In other cases, the therapist may work in a health-related rather than a medical institution, such as a child care or senior citizen center. In these cases an occupational therapist may be working without a physician's referral. Here the treatment program will be planned in relation to the goals of the institution, the needs of the individual patient or client, and in collaboration with the personnel of the agency.

In an educational setting, the therapist works collaboratively with the teaching and other health care personnel present, establishing goals for each individual through the team process. Treatment programs in schools focus on needs of the children with respect to education-related benefits.

TEAMWORK

A rehabilitation team is multidisciplinary, with each member contributing specialized educational background and expertise. This sharing of different viewpoints leads to more comprehensive problem solving with regard to the patient or client, who is also considered a vital member of the team when feasible. Family members also may play an important role in the team process.

As indicated, a wide variety of professionals work together to offer the most effective aid to help people mobilize their own resources. All team members are concerned with the welfare of the patient or client. It is important for the occupational therapist to coordinate efforts with all of the personnel who are working toward the rehabilitation of each patient or client. This is the total rehabilitation team. The number and types of professional services vary considerably according to each individual's overall needs.

It is most important that the rehabilitation team work effectively together. This is accomplished through staff meetings, circulated reports, and other collaborative efforts.

The Physician

In a medical or institutional setting the patient's physician, regardless of specialty, becomes the coordinator of the treatment process. The physician may be a neurologist, orthopedist, surgeon, internist, physiatrist (a doctor of physical medicine), pediatrician, or a practitioner of other medical specialties.

The Nurse

The hospital nurse is responsible for the patient's care twenty-four hours a day. He or she must see to the patient's bodily care and comfort, meals, medication, and appointments with other departments, such as X-ray, surgery, laboratory, and physical and occupational therapy. In addition, the nurse often is the person in charge of the unit and is kept informed regarding the patients. No patient ever should leave or be taken from the ward without the knowledge of the nurse in charge of that patient's care.

The Social Worker

The social worker can be the professional liaison between the patient, the family, and the physician or other health care worker. The social worker, through interviewing, obtains a history that includes pertinent information needed to understand the patient's particular situation. For example, educational level, family and community relationships, beliefs and attitudes, home situation, and employment history might be of importance. Financial status determines whether financial assistance should be sought. Assistance is given in working out financial problems.

In some settings (for example, counseling centers, drug and alcohol abuse treatment centers, and some psychiatric treatment facilities) social workers may conduct extensive individual and group counseling. In almost all inpatient or residential facilities, social workers help in planning the transition from the facility to the community or the transfer to another facility.

The Physical Therapist

The physical therapist evaluates and treats movement dysfunctions of anatomic or physiologic origin, to maximize health and function. Problems in the musculoskeletal, neurological, cardiovascular, and pulmonary systems are treated, and individual therapists often have specialized areas of competence that influence their caseloads. Exercise, massage, ambulation training, and other techniques may be used to accomplish goals. Modalities including hydrotherapy, ultrasound, and diathermy also might be used during specific treatment programs.

As with all of the health professions, some physical therapists engage in research, consultation, or education. Physical therapy assistants work under the direct supervision of a physical therapist to help carry out treatment programs.

The Vocational Counselor

The vocational counselor is a necessary part of the team when there is a need to plan a new vocational objective for the patient or client. The counselor accumulates information regarding capabilities, limitations and aptitudes, interests, and skills. Information is provided by the counselor concerning the various vocations that are possible despite the disability. Once a vocational objective is reached, plans are made for any necessary training, assistance in finding employment is given, and follow-up is carried out to determine work adjustment.

The Psychologist

The psychologist usually has two broad functions: aiding the patient in adjustment and collecting diagnostic information. He or she helps to alleviate emotional problems that do not require medication. The psychologist obtains diagnostic information by testing intelligence, interests, aptitudes, and personality. These tests yield information that is helpful to other professionals also treating the individual. In the event that there is no vocational counselor on the staff, the psychologist in some settings assumes these responsibilities.

The Speech-Language Pathologist

The speech-language pathologist evaluates individuals with dysfunctional language or speech and provides treatment for such problems. Some speech-language clinicians also evaluate and treat difficulties associated with eating that involve the musculature of the mouth and swallowing.

The Therapeutic Recreation Specialist

The therapeutic recreation specialist plans for the recreational needs of patients. Programs may be entirely group oriented or they may be developed according to the needs of each individual within the group. Usually, a combination of these two approaches is found. Recreation plans may include movies, dances, outings, concerts, special holiday events, opportunities for religious worship, sports, games, and music programs. Programs include both active and passive participation.

Working Together

All therapeutic programming must be carefully coordinated and must work toward the same objectives for the patient or client. This requires preplanning and the clearance of many schedules.

The occupational therapist, therefore, must plan in terms of the total program of several or many other disciplines. No single professional can do a total job of rehabilitation, as each has a proper place and must recognize the contribution of other disciplines. Total health care requires that all disciplines work together to promote the patient's return to the community.

CHAPTER 2

DEVELOPMENT OF THE OCCUPATIONAL THERAPY FIELD

The profession of occupational therapy has its roots in the development of psychiatry and in the philosophy of treatment of the mentally ill. Several centuries ago, patients with mental disturbances were not understood as sick persons, but were thought to be under a spell or possessed by demons. In many instances, these individuals were beaten, put in chains and imprisoned in cells, or left to die.

It was not until the eighteenth century that the progressive thinking of a few doctors in Spain, France, England, Germany, and later in the United States, removed these sick people from their imprisonment and isolation and put them to work. They were assigned to various tasks concerned with the maintenance of the institution. In addition, musical concerts, lectures, rides through the countryside, etc., were provided, and classes were designed to give instruction in educational subjects and in manual activities.

To the surprise of all concerned, many patients who were assigned to diversified activity programs not only got well faster, they often recovered completely. There are numerous fascinating records concerned with the growing recognition of the therapeutic values of activity therapy during the latter part of the eighteenth and throughout the nineteenth centuries.

Occupations used as treatment for mentally ill patients began a new concept of health care that spread rapidly in Western Europe and the United States. In the early 1800s aides were used in carrying out this new concept in the management of mentally ill patients in the various hospital industries, such as farming, dairy work, laundry, clerical work, and housekeeping. Eventually teachers and instructors were employed in the hospitals that utilized work programs of this kind, but these personnel lacked a background in psychology and medicine. Dr. Herbert Hall was among the first to recognize this need during the early part of the twentieth century. He employed highly skilled instructors in the arts and crafts and taught them about anatomy, physiology, and psychology. He also began the systematic use of occupations for treatment by developing a series of progressive steps to serve the physical or mental needs of his patients. In 1906, a nurse in Boston, Susan Tracy, gave a course to nurses in "Invalid Occupations." There followed in different parts of the United States several courses of this kind. This was the beginning.

As early as 1912, in an article published by Dr. Von Rondburg of Germany, this claim was advanced:

> As a physician, it is my prerogative to draw emphatic attention to the not yet sufficiently appreciated advantages of occupations for the afflicted, both mental and physical. The close intervening of the psychic functions with the somatic processes makes medical treatment without sufficient consideration of both aspects unthinkable.

Today, this consideration of both psychic functions and somatic processes underlies the basic philosophy of occupational therapy.

A YOUNG PROFESSION: 1917–44

In 1917, a small group of people met and formed an association, The National Society for the Promotion of Occupational Therapy, later incorporated as The American Occupational Therapy Association (AOTA). George Edward Barton, a founding member, was responsible for originating the term *occupational therapy,* and Dr. H. A. Pattison presented the infant organization with this first official definition: "Occupational therapy may be defined as any activity, mental or physical, definitely prescribed for the distinct purpose of contributing to and hastening recovery from disease or injury."

World War I

With the entrance of the United States into World War I in 1917, the Surgeon General of the U.S. Army requested occupational therapists for overseas service and ordered the establishment of three-month training courses to train "reconstruction aides." Following World War I, doctors who had used this form of treatment with war-injured patients overseas requested its use in civilian hospitals. Thus, occupational therapy began to emerge as a definite professional adjunct to medicine in the management of a variety of disabilities, including both mental and physical disabilities.

The Establishment of Standards

Minimum standards for the training of occupational therapists were developed in 1922, based at first on three-month courses that were established in Boston, Philadelphia, and St. Louis. Courses were expanded until the 1940s, when all programs were established in four-year colleges and universities within the framework of baccalaureate degree programs. In 1935, the American Medical Association undertook the evaluation and approval of educational programs in occupational therapy. This has been a joint process with The American Occupational Therapy Association.

In order to protect patients and therapists, a registration procedure for qualified therapists was established in 1936 by the American Occupational Therapy Association. This led to the development of standards for practice and the assessment of individuals to meet those standards. Certification by successful completion of a national examination was established in 1946. Organizational changes in 1986 led to the formation of the American Occupational Therapy Certification Board, which now issues the certificates.

World War II

When mobilization for a second world war began, the occupational therapy profession was ill-prepared to meet the urgent personnel demands that were to be made. There were approximately nine hundred registered therapists in the country to be divided between civilian hospitals and those of the armed forces. Many new schools were developed, shortened War Emergency courses were organized, and a large volunteer corps was trained. Working with the war-injured expanded the knowledge and skill of therapists in working with severely handicapped patients. This was a period of specialization, when therapists developed skills in working with various orthopedic, neurological, and other injuries, and first became involved in making orthotic devices, such as assistive splints.

EXPANSION AND CONSOLIDATION: 1945–64

Expansion continued following World War II with emphasis on rehabilitation of the chronic diseases of an aging population, such as arthritis, cancer, heart disease, stroke, and other diseases of the nervous system. A new philosophy was developing as the process of the multidisciplinary team approach to treatment was recognized as essential to quality patient care. During this period therapists also began practicing in the public school system.

This new approach was greatly aided by the impetus of state and federal legislation that supported the development of health programs by funding the construction of rehabilitation facilities and traineeships for students in education.

Standards for occupational therapy education were strengthened when The American Occupational Therapy Association undertook an intensive three-year curriculum analysis. This study was directed toward:

1. A job analysis of the profession.
2. A curriculum analysis of the educational programs.
3. A matching of the instructional patterns against job demands to determine the functional status of curricula.

The results led to many educational actions and changes, such as holding annual workshops for educators and the development of behavioral objectives for educational programs. Another outgrowth of this project was the plan to initiate entry-level programs at the master's level for students who had completed baccalaureates in other fields.

The World Federation of Occupational Therapists was founded in 1952, when representatives from ten national organizations, The American Occupational Therapy Association being one, met and drew up by-laws and educational standards for all member countries. Seven years later the World Federation of Occupational Therapists affiliated as a nongovernmental organization with the World Health Organization, which is dedicated to promoting high standards of health throughout the world (see also Chapter 5).

The young profession continued to be plagued by personnel shortages, there never having been a sufficient number of schools to educate the number of therapists needed. Another factor that kept the numbers of practicing therapists down was the attrition rate to marriage and raising a family, since the profession had historically been dominated by women. During the 1940s, men began entering the field in increasing numbers.

In an effort to extend these limited personnel resources, in 1958 the American Occupational Therapy Association endorsed the education of occupational therapy assistants. Once again, educational standards were established and a system for accrediting schools and for certifying graduates was planned. This has been a highly successful undertaking and certified occupational therapy assistants (COTAs) are making valuable contributions to patient and educational programs.

In 1964, the AOTA authorized the formation of a foundation. The American Occupational Therapy Foundation is organized exclusively for charitable scientific, literary, and educational purposes. The foundation has: provided scholarships and fellowships; supported special studies, surveys, and research; and published monographs, visual aids, and special reports.

CONTINUED GROWTH: 1965–87

Phenomenal growth has occurred during the past 35 years in occupational therapy. Thousands of new therapists enter the field each year, and still the demand for services grows. New areas of need calling for the skills and theoretical knowledge of occupational therapists continue to emerge. As quality health care has become increasingly available to more of the population, expansion has occurred in traditional areas and new service delivery systems have developed.

In the 1960s, community mental health centers came into existence to treat emotionally ill persons in their home communities rather than at a few large state or private institutions. In the same decade, Medicare became a reality, providing a federally sponsored health insurance program for elderly persons. Medicaid also was developed as a federally sponsored, state-administered program for those with low incomes. Occupational therapists were needed along with other health professionals to provide services for people covered under these plans.

In the 1970s, Public Law 94–142, mandating education for all handicapped children, caused public schools to hire large numbers of related services personnel, including occupational therapists, to meet the needs of children with all types of disabling conditions.

By this decade medical knowledge also had shown astounding growth, and relevant new information was used by occupational therapists to improve their treatment. Many new health-related businesses sprang up to provide equipment and supplies for diagnosis and treatment. Occupational therapists benefited from the manufacture of adapted equipment that once had to be made by hand (examples include eating aids, wheelchair adaptations, and therapy equipment of all types). Splints of certain kinds became available in graduated sizes and improved materials, relieving occupational therapists of the need to design and cut every splint individually.

With the increase in the number of therapists over the years and the variety of specialty areas in which occupational therapists work, a need for greater sharing of information was perceived. Professional groups made up of therapists from a number of occupational therapy specialty areas initiated newsletters for members and began holding meetings at the state and national levels to share issues, concerns, and up-to-date information. A national student association also developed, giving students a combined voice and a means of sharing and growing in their chosen profession.

The increase in the number of therapists, and the growing trend toward obtaining master's and doctoral degrees, led to a proliferation of new books and journals. These factors added impetus to the study of the profession's philosophical bases. Research became of great importance as therapists sought to validate theory and practice. With more therapists obtaining postbaccalaureate degrees, research skills began to be used more in clinical situations. Skills in research methods are of great practical value in studying the effects of treatment to ensure quality of care.

Licensing of occupational therapists within states has increased so that almost all states now have such laws in place. These laws protect both the public and the therapists.

DIVERSITY AND GROWTH: 1988–2000

Occupational therapists held about sixty thousand jobs in 1998. The U.S. Bureau of Labor Statistics has predicted a 55 percent increase in job openings by 2006. Clearly it is a growing and dynamic field.

The expansion of the profession and the resultant greater visibility of its practitioners, along with efforts by The American Occupational Therapy Association and state associations to educate the public about occupational therapy, have created increased demand for services as well as a tremendous increase in the number of students seeking admission to academic programs. Many colleges and universities have added programs, with occupational therapy now being offered at more than two hundred colleges and universities in the United States, including the District of Columbia and Puerto Rico.

Growth has brought diversity. Occupational therapists have a wide variety of job choices with excellent salaries and benefits. Salaries for occupational therapists and occupational therapy assistants have risen substantially over the years (see Chapter 6 for specific salary levels).

Interest in specialization and in gaining recognition for expertise in various practice areas or treatment techniques appears to have increased. Therapists, for example, might seek pediatric certification, or certified hand therapist status, or certification in neurodevelopmental therapy. More than half of the registered therapists surveyed in the past ten years considered themselves to be specialists rather than generalists, whether or not they had any specialty certification. Therapists often assume a primary role in a treatment area and therefore "specialize" in it. In addition, approximately one-third of OTRs and almost one-quarter of COTAs consider "consultation" their secondary employment function.

As one reflects on the history of occupational therapy, it can be seen that amazing growth has occurred in the relatively short existence of the profession. The years ahead are expected to bring additional quality changes.

FUTURE OF THE PROFESSION

What does the future hold for the profession of occupational therapy in terms of practice? The American Occupational Therapy Association interviewed leaders in the profession to obtain their perspective. Some leaders believe that occupational therapists will work in increasingly diverse settings in both medical and nonmedical areas, including ergonomics, driver rehabilitation and training, welfare-to-work services, and health and wellness consulting. The greater life expectancy of Americans will increase the need for therapists working with the elderly, and the greater awareness among parents of disabled children of the services available will increase the demand for pediatric occupational therapists working in hospitals, schools, homes, and nursing homes. Rehabilitation is effective in returning workers to their jobs after injury sooner and in better physical condition than without skilled intervention, and employers and insurers will no doubt value the cost-effectiveness of such services and increasingly make use of them. In the area of mental health, we will see efforts by The American Occupational Therapy Association to promote therapist interest and practice in this once primary area of occupational therapy.

There will be a need in the profession for scholars and clinician researchers who can provide the research base necessary for practice. New treatments developed from theory will evolve, and current treatments will remain or be eliminated based on their effectiveness, as proven or disproven through research.

Despite all the anticipated changes, emphasis on "function" is expected to remain as a core concept in occupational therapy. Occupational therapists will continue to work to improve performance deficits.

Ethical practice will be addressed more closely in the health professions, just as it is being addressed in business, government, and other areas of our society.

Occupational therapists will be encouraged to take an active role in related organizations at the local, state, national, and international levels, so that they may be advocates for the profession and for the consumers of its services. Occupational therapists will need to be aware of how their service delivery fits within the total system of which it is a part, including the total health care system and systems specific to each practice setting.

Rapid changes are occurring in the health care system, and the future under the anticipated national health care reform cannot be accurately predicted. If the goal of improved access to health care, including occupational therapy services, is reached, then the need for therapists may expand even more than presently predicted.

HEALTH CARE AND PREVENTION

The past several years have witnessed the emergence of new emphases and thrusts in the area of health care delivery. Occupational therapy had previously functioned largely within the medical model of patient care, with primary emphasis on treatment and recovery following illness or injury. This emphasis is still strong, but other philosophies of health care delivery are emerging.

Health, rather than illness, has now become the key word, with effort directed toward the prevention of dysfunction and the maintenance of function. Thus, the community model of health care delivery has been established with services frequently offered in patient homes and in community centers, rather than in the hospital. Services are needed in mental health crisis centers, senior citizen facilities, halfway houses, outpatient rehabilitation departments, nursery schools, educational institutions, and the public school systems.

In the area of patient care, much attention is now directed toward the early identification of learning and developmental problems requiring sensory, cognitive, motor, and social stimulation through various techniques of occupational therapy. Care of the aging in community centers, nursing homes, and continued care facilities has become a major area of specialization.

The need to evaluate the efficiency of both clinical and educational programs has led to increasing research. As questions are identified, an organized methodology is being employed in the search for answers.

Occupational therapy is responding to changing societal needs and to rapid advances in health care technology. Members of the profession are contributing to the knowledge explosion in unique, creative, and beneficial ways.

The years from 1917 to 2000 have witnessed the maturation of an idea and philosophy into a fully developed profession. This is a proud heritage of hard work and accomplishment. Occupational therapy provides a service to society. The profession has a unique body of knowledge increasingly documented by research and established standards of practice as well as a code of ethics. A strong national association allows for leadership and direction.

CHAPTER 3

THE OCCUPATIONAL THERAPY PROCESS

Occupational therapists work with individuals who have conditions that are mentally, physically, developmentally, or emotionally disabling. They help them develop, recover, or maintain daily living and work skills. The goal of occupational therapists is to help their clients have independent, satisfying, and productive lives.

These clients often seek occupational therapy services on their own or they may be referred by physicians or other professionals. The need for a physician's referral is apparent in medical settings. The logical sequence of steps in determining and meeting patient or client needs is called the *occupational therapy process*. It consists of: screening, evaluation, treatment planning, treatment implementation, and reevaluation. Careful thought and problem-solving skills are required throughout.

SCREENING

In the screening phase the occupational therapist customarily determines important information about the patient's or client's condition. Access to records of any prior or current health care, interviewing of the individual, and brief screening tests are some of the methods employed in learning about the status and potential for benefit from available services. The screening part of the process is a general stage rather than a specific detail-finding stage. Major areas investigated might include a rough estimate of developmental level (particularly in a child or developmentally disabled adult), ability to carry out daily living skills or work responsibilities, and ability to engage in meaningful leisure activities.

The occupational therapist attempts to determine specific areas that will require further evaluation and to estimate length of treatment required, if possible. Records of findings and interpretations must be kept for documentation purposes. Recommendations are made for further action or referral based on available services. It may be necessary to consult with a team social worker or with other health professionals and agencies to seek help if there is a lack of financial resources for necessary care.

The Certified Occupational Therapy Assistant (COTA), supervised by a Registered Occupational Therapist (OTR), may assist in the screening process by performing such necessary tasks as obtaining data from medical charts, interviewing relatives, and carrying out some measurements.

EVALUATION

Evaluation involves in-depth gathering of data in the specific areas needed for planning and implementing treatment. The therapist attempts to find reasons for deficiencies in functioning in the life areas of self-care, work, and play or leisure activities. Factors interfering with life functioning can be physical, cognitive, emotional, or social, and it is the task of the occupational therapist to investigate problem areas carefully so as to implement effective treatment that will help the patient or client return to satisfying, productive, and maximally independent living.

The methods used in evaluation include some of those used during screening, but they are more thoroughly utilized, and other investigative means can be employed as well. In addition to interviewing and reading records for information about the previous medical, social, and employment history, formal tests and measurements and structured observations may be used. Specific areas evaluated depend upon the individual patient's or client's problem areas and the particular therapist's area of practice. Some common areas evaluated include musculoskeletal status, sensory integration capabilities, physical or psychological daily living skills, cognition, psychological (emotional) status, social or interpersonal relationships, and potential for return to work.

Data gathered must be documented and interpreted, and often a formal report is sent to the referring source. The report usually takes into consideration the individual's abilities as well as disabilities—both physical and emotional—his or her interpersonal support systems, and personal motivation toward independence. The COTA, under OTR supervision, may be involved in some areas of the evaluation, as, for example, the daily living skills area, joint range-of-motion and muscle-strength testing, and wheelchair mobility status.

TREATMENT PLAN

In the treatment planning phase, the registered occupational therapist uses evaluation results to formulate prioritized goals and develop treatment objectives that specify means for achieving goals in step-by-step fashion. When possible, the therapist works with the patient or client to set goals of personal value to that individual. The objectives identify the approach, methods, techniques, and media to be used. The certified occupational therapy assistant is an integral part of this process, since in many areas he or she may be guiding the patient or client through treatment.

Tasks and treatment methods involving as much active participation of the patient or client as possible are selected to fulfill the treatment plan. Treatment is designed to bring about the desired improvements and reach goals set in physical, developmental, emotional, social, or cognitive areas. The OTR and COTA have been trained to analyze activities for their component parts and their possible value in achieving goals. For example, an activity can be analyzed for the specific movements and muscle use involved, for the types of cognitive processes required, for the stimulating or sedating nature of the task, for the interpersonal reactions that might be elicited, etc.

IMPLEMENTATION OF TREATMENT

In implementing the treatment plan, occupational therapists may use many means to help the patient or client reach the goals that were developed. They use verbal means to guide and teach, encourage, motivate, and provide feedback regarding general behavior or specific performance. They must think creatively to solve problems of individuals and lead them to triumph over mental or physical disabilities.

The use of activities in treatment allows the patient or client to be involved in his or her own habilitation or rehabilitation in a participatory way. Active involvement in purposeful activities to fulfill goals is believed to be the primary way by which human beings learn, change, and attain life satisfaction. Activities may be used with individuals and with groups. Work, play, sports, games, crafts, exercise through task participation, food preparation, computer use, and many other life activities may be used to meet specific goals of a physical, psychological, or developmental nature.

Sometimes preliminary splinting, neuromuscular facilitation techniques, or exercise with or without equipment may be used before a physically disabled individual can participate to any extent in life activities. However, the goal of all treatment in occupational therapy is to reach independence in the highest possible degree. Developing strength, endurance, range of motion, and coordination may be goals.

In some cases adaptations must be made to items in the environment that will allow a person more independence and greater comfort. Sometimes a simple attachment to a commonly used item (such as a spoon, hairbrush, or pencil) will make it usable, while other adaptations may be quite complex. Therapists may work with rehabilitation engineers to design equipment. Communication and learning may be enhanced through adapting computers and typewriters. Techniques of body use to maximize strength and mobility may free a person from dependence on others for dressing, transferring from bed to wheelchair, and so forth. Work simplification techniques may be taught to conserve energy. Adaptations along with training may allow greater personal freedom, as with special wheelchairs or through automobile training with the use of hand controls or other adaptations that permit driving despite a physical disability.

Assertiveness training or stress management techniques may lead to a sense of well being and greater control; a group activity in which everyone must work together and interrelate well enough to accomplish the task affords an excellent opportunity for an individual not only to gain insight into his or her behavior but also to use such a setting as a laboratory for attempting new behaviors. Field trips out of a facility may be used to encourage re-entry into the community by providing opportunities for head-injured or long-term mentally ill persons to relearn the skills that are needed for taking public transportation, buying grocery items, and learning to carry out a sequence of steps in everyday tasks.

As can be seen from the above descriptions, occupational therapy treatment might take many forms, including many not mentioned here. For a person who likes challenge and reward in making other people's lives better, occupational therapy is an excellent career choice.

REEVALUATION

Reevaluation at intervals during the course of treatment helps the therapist determine progress and ensure effective, quality care. Results might indicate that the current treatment is producing the desired changes, or that an alternative treatment plan should be developed. It also might indicate that maximum benefits have been achieved and that treatment may be discontinued. Maximum benefits may not necessarily mean that the individual has achieved full function, but only that further treatment is unwarranted at the present time. When treatment is discontinued, the therapist must make certain that arrangements are made for any necessary follow-up care or referrals.

TREATMENT AREAS

Occupational therapy intervention is directed toward the alleviation of actual or potential loss of function in one or more spheres of life: physical, emotional, social, and vocational. In the following discussion of treatment areas, try to visualize how the separate areas combine and overlap to form a unique treatment program for each patient or client.

Physical Dysfunction

Many diseases affect muscles so that they do not act reciprocally as they should; these muscles are referred to as uncoordinated. Here, exercises are given to improve coordination and enable the patient to perform motions correctly and smoothly. Techniques for applying sensory stimulation to skin, muscles, and joints (for example, stroking, tapping, pressure, or joint movement) may be used to encourage improved voluntary movement and task performance.

Some patients who will never again use a paralyzed arm or leg must, nevertheless, be taught to care for themselves. They must learn to live with the use of perhaps only two extremities (limbs), and to use their residual abilities in spite of their handicaps. When full restoration or correction of a patient's physical problems is impossible, the occupational therapist may teach compensation techniques.

Another type of patient that the therapist works with is the one who has sustained an amputation and must learn to use an artificial leg or arm. The occupational therapist employs a range of daily living skills techniques for this kind of patient and teaches him or her how to work with the prosthesis. Skill in use of the prosthesis encourages the greater independence of the patient.

For some patients, the therapist utilizes procedures that will increase the circulation of blood to the injured area, for this in itself may hasten the healing process.

The occupational therapist works with children and adults with cerebral palsy and contributes a great deal in this field. These are neurologically impaired individuals who may have defects of motor control and speech, hearing, or visual problems. Physical habilitation is carried out through neuromuscular techniques, traditional exercise, and daily living skills training. Adaptive devices for self-care, communication, and play are selected or designed to meet individual needs. For example, one child might need adapted utensils for self-feeding or a computer adaptation for learning, communication, and fun. When working with handicapped children, one must never forget that they are children first, with children's psychological and social needs.

Children with cerebral palsy and other disabling conditions must be provided experiences that give them the sensory input they do not receive through most children's customary play activities. They also must be given as many skills as possible to make their lives less frustrating and more independent and satisfying.

Regardless of the diagnosis, emotional reactions of the patient are inevitable. Whether the occupational therapist is treating a person with an orthopedic problem, a heart condition, or a spinal cord injury, the therapist is treating the patient as a total person and considers psychological needs and responses in addition to the physical problems. A well-planned occupational therapy program can prevent problems before they arise as well as alleviate any problems that may develop.

Psychosocial Dysfunction

Therapists working in psychiatric settings may work with patients exhibiting psychotic behaviors as a result of such illnesses as schizophrenia, bipolar disorder (manic-depressive psychosis), or paranoia. In those settings and in community-based facilities serving less severely disturbed individuals, occupational therapists may work with persons demonstrating anxiety, drug and alcohol problems, dysthymic disorders (neuroses), disturbances caused by transient life situations, and so on. Occupational therapists also may work to promote mental health in wellness programs, providing guidance to alleviate stress, increase coping skills, improve self-concept, and so forth. Guidance to improve skills for successful interpersonal relationships may help patients or clients become more comfortable with themselves and more satisfied with their lives. Activities are carefully chosen to develop and enhance successful behaviors.

Occupational therapy for the emotionally ill may be directed toward the following goals:

1. To reinforce mental health through teaching the patient, family, or other caregivers to structure the environment in which the patient lives and works.
2. To evaluate a patient's ability to relate to other people.
3. To plan and carry out treatment programs designed to influence the emotional disorder in a positive way.
4. To contribute to the social and vocational adjustment of the patient in his or her community.

In order to do this, the therapist must have an understanding of the meaning of behavior and of the dynamics of human relationships. It is a goal of occupational therapists working in psychiatric facilities to provide a therapeutic environment that will aid recovery. With this understanding the occupational therapist is able to plan specific therapy programs designed to encourage independent living, vocational readiness, and social competence.

Social Objectives

Socially, the therapist has a valuable contribution to make to humankind, for each person is basically a social being. The skills of occupational therapy have a significant social meaning.

The patient is encouraged to participate in social activity, to see herself or himself as a contributing member of the group rather than as one set apart. The patient is aided to realize her or his abilities in meeting the demands of the social order.

More generally, the therapist has a responsibility to the community at large. One of the social objectives of occupational therapy is to assist the patient in coping with disability and to understand his or her potential despite that disability. This state of social readiness, of returning to an active community role, is fostered by the occupational therapist.

Vocational Evaluation

Prevocational exploration and vocational evaluation have achieved a prominent place in the total rehabilitation of the patient. By definition, prevocational exploration implies an early screening and evaluation process to ascertain the patient's work tolerance, physical strength, and ability to meet the demands of the work situation. This prevocational exploration of basic work skills, work habits, motivation, and interests is recorded on evaluation record forms. The occupational therapist then acts as an evaluator of the general skills of the patient or client and of his or her specific vocational skills.

The therapist also assists with special problems of work adaptation, interpreting performance difficulties to work supervisors and providing the supportive link between medical rehabilitation and job placement.

The rehabilitation process must be oriented to the total needs of the patient, be they medical, psychological, social, or vocational. Even in a strictly medical setting there is the need for initial vocational planning. In some occupational therapy skill activities, careful observation of the patient or client can give important job-related information regarding work habits, temperament or emotional stability, interests, and manual dexterity.

Essentially, the vocational evaluation process consists of skills analysis, activity observation, physical capacities evaluation, and exploration of work potential through job samples and aptitude tests. This process is followed by the occupational therapist's recommendations and a final report of findings to the vocational counselor and any referring physician or agency. Vocational training and actual job placement are usually handled by persons with industrial experience and placement training.

ECONOMIC FACTORS

Economically, therapists have a part to play in hastening recovery of patients, thereby decreasing the time lost at work. Many occupational therapists in hospitals, rehabilitation facilities, and private practice incorporate work programs and functional capacities evaluations into their programs. Some provide consultation to business and industry representatives regarding methods of preventing consistently recurring injuries that result from repetitive or overly stressful physical tasks.

Today a number of insurance companies refer industrial accident cases to rehabilitation units for treatment, including both occupational and physical therapy. The time saved in recovery, and, therefore, in compensation, far outweighs the expense of treatment.

During wartime, the medical departments of the armed forces found this same concept to be valid, and early, intensive treatment by rehabilitation techniques saved many lost work hours.

CHAPTER 4

ENTERING THE PROFESSION: EDUCATION, CERTIFICATION, AND PERSONAL ATTRIBUTES

This chapter will detail the requirements needed to enter the field at the professional and assistant levels. Both qualifications (for occupational therapist and occupational therapy assistant) have entry-level requirements concerned with: (1) educational preparation leading to qualification by The American Occupational Therapy Association; (2) personal qualifications including individual characteristics, interests, and attributes; and (3) health requirements, both physical and emotional.

EDUCATION

Education includes an understanding of life tasks and skills, interpersonal relationships, social roles, and human functions. The educational foundation needed by the student should be developed through a strong background of college preparatory work in high school and should continue with liberal arts and science courses in college. Courses may include English composition, literature and speech, biological science, natural sciences, psychology, sociology, history, foreign language, art, and mathematics.

You should enrich your experience by participating in extracurricular activities to develop hobbies and interests as well as to meet many different kinds of people. You need to enjoy being with people, to develop a sensitivity to and an appreciation for the needs of others. You should develop your communication skills, both written and oral, as well as the nonverbal skills. You need problem-solving and decision-making skills. You must be able to analyze and interpret. Only as much as you understand yourself, your strengths and weaknesses, and your philosophy of life, can you be helpful to others in regaining lost patterns of behavior. Students currently in occupational therapy educational programs recommend gaining firsthand experience of occupational therapy through visiting clinical programs and volunteering or working as occupational therapy aides.

Registered Occupational Therapist (OTR)

To qualify as a registered occupational therapist (OTR), the minimum of a bachelor's degree in occupational therapy is required. Programs leading to this degree are usually four years in length and include approximately two years of liberal arts, two years of professional studies, and six to nine months of supervised clinical field practice. For students who already hold a baccalaureate in a related field, there are graduate programs in occupational therapy that prepare one for entry-level qualification. Some professional entry-level master's degree programs admit students with at least ninety undergraduate semester hours and appropriate prerequisites or senior status. Programs leading to a postbaccalaureate certificate usually include two semesters of academic work and six months of supervised practice. Other programs lead to a master's degree and include three to four semesters of academic work and a minimum of six months of practice. It should be noted that schools vary in their curriculum and practice requirements.

(See Appendix C for a list of accredited programs in occupational therapy.)

At this writing, baccalaureate or master's educational programs in occupational therapy to prepare graduates for entry-level positions exist in more than 140 colleges and universities in this country, including the District of Columbia and Puerto Rico. These programs are accredited by the Accreditation Council for Occupational Therapy Education of The American Occupational Therapy Association (4720 Montgomery Lane, Bethesda, MD 20814; 301-652-AOTA; www.aota.org).

ADMISSION REQUIREMENTS

Specific admission requirements are established by the individual colleges and universities. As soon as you have established a career plan and identified potential colleges or universities, it is important to determine the admission requirements that you must be prepared to meet at the college of your choice. The following will give you some idea of the range of subjects.

If you are in high school and are planning a career in occupational therapy, the following is a list of the subjects generally required to enter college or university programs with a major in occupational therapy.

Courses
biology, chemistry, or physics
English
history or social studies
mathematics

A human growth and development course is required by many programs, and a basic statistics course may be required, particularly if you wish to begin an entry-level master's program.

If you are in college and want to transfer to an occupational therapy program, the following requirements have been compiled from accredited curricula in occupational therapy. Prerequisites for specific programs may be obtained by writing to those programs (see Appendix C).

Courses
biological and/or natural sciences
English
psychology, abnormal psychology, developmental psychology
sociology or anthropology

ENTRY-LEVEL PROFESSIONAL EDUCATION

An ideal entry-level educational program is outlined in a handout entitled "The Essentials and Guidelines for an Accredited Educational Program for the Occupational Therapist," published by The American Occupational Therapy Association. All accredited programs follow the same basic outline, although variations in emphasis are found in each program, depending upon the curriculum within the university or college. All programs prepare students to become competent, resourceful therapists with the necessary competencies and skills to carry out the required professional functions. The following curriculum areas and objectives serve as the basis of all educational programs:

• *Liberal arts content* is prerequisite to or concurrent with professional education. It will facilitate communication skills, logical thinking, critical analysis, problem solving, and creativity. Liberal arts content also is important in developing ability to make judgments based on broad background knowledge, and in developing multicultural knowledge and appreciation.

• *Biological, behavioral and health sciences content,* prerequisite to or concurrent with professional education, encompasses normal and abnormal conditions throughout the life span. Courses include anatomy, physiology, neurosciences, and kinesiology. Other courses include content on human development and behavior; congenital, developmental, acute, and chronic disease processes and traumatic injuries, and their effect on human functioning; and effects of health and disability on individuals, families, and society.

• *Occupational therapy theory and practice content* includes the foundations and historical and philosophical bases of the profession, and the theoretical bases and models of practice. It also includes fundamentals of activity, such as the analysis, teaching, and adapting of activities of daily living, work, and play/leisure. The occupational therapy process, based on frames of reference or theoretical perspectives, is studied in-depth, and documentation of services through appropriate record keeping also is covered.

• *Occupational therapy service management content* is designed to develop ability to apply principles of management in providing services. Among other things, methods of planning, organizing, staffing, and coordinating are taught, and students learn about factors important in health care delivery.

• *Research content* includes the value of research in clinical practice and professional development, components of research protocols, and interpretation and application of research study results.

• *Professional ethics content* is important in guiding therapists' conduct so that professional standards and ethics are respected and the profession is appropriately maintained and promoted.

• *Fieldwork education* is required. Level I fieldwork is clinical experience obtained during the academic course-work semesters, giving students a better perspective for learning clinical applications of theories and techniques. Level II fieldwork consists of a minimum of six months' of supervised full-time experience in clinical settings.

Certified Occupational Therapy Assistant (COTA)

Two types of entry-level programs can be identified for personnel at the assistant level: those leading to a certificate are usually twelve to fourteen months in length; those leading to an associate degree are usually two years long. Programs are established in technical and vocational institutes, junior and community colleges, and four-year colleges (see Appendix C).

Admission requirements for entry into these programs include graduation from an accredited high school, or the equivalent, and specific course prerequisites similar to those cited earlier for the professional level.

The occupational therapy assistant educational program is outlined in "The Essentials and Guidelines for an Accredited Educational Program for the Occupational Therapy Assistant," as adopted by the American Medical Association and The American Occupational Therapy Association. The program includes classroom work and required fieldwork. Content includes the following:

• *General education* that is prerequisite to or concurrent with technical education and that facilitates communication skills, problem-solving, and knowledge and appreciation of multicultural factors.

• *Biological, behavioral, and health sciences,* prerequisite to or concurrent with technical education, encompass normal and abnormal conditions that may occur throughout the life span. Information gained in this content area includes knowledge about the human body and conditions treated in occupational therapy. Students learn about human behavior, community and environmental effects on the individual, and influences affecting health.

• *Occupational therapy principles and practice skills* area includes the underlying foundation, history, and philosophical bases of the profession; an emphasis on the use of purposeful activities and occupation for enhancing role function; and fundamentals of analyzing, teaching, and adapting activities of daily living, work, and play/leisure. The occupational therapy process (screening and assessment, treatment planning, implementation, reassessment, and termination) includes learning about assessment and intervention methods and collaborating with the certified occupational therapist in intervention. The occupational therapy assistant student also learns about management of services, directing activity programs, documenting services, and communicating with others. In addition, the occupational therapy assistant develops values, attitudes, and behaviors that are necessary not only to maintain the profession's standards and ethics but to enhance the assistant's roles in the profession.

• *Fieldwork education* consists of two phases. Level I fieldwork provides experiences that enhance classroom learning through observation and participation in basic aspects of the occupational therapy process. Level II fieldwork, for which the minimum requirement is twelve weeks of full-time experience, provides indepth experience needed to gain entry-level competency for occupational therapy practice at the assistant level.

Some associate degree programs link into four-year baccalaureate programs, thereby enabling the assistant who is seeking career advancement to continue to the professional level without too much loss of time. A COTA desiring OTR preparation also might consider professional entry-level master's degree programs, some of which allow admission with a minimum of ninety undergraduate semester hours (equivalent to about three years of college work). These programs require sufficient credit hours at the master's level to balance out the fewer undergraduate credits.

GRADUATE AND CONTINUING EDUCATION

Any student entering the health professions today must recognize that education is a lifelong process. You will never know all there is to know, for our educational horizons are continually broadening. As you work with new ideas, you come to understand different dimensions of problems, ask more questions, and seek more answers.

Continuing education enables you to learn more about a specific function in a short period of time: a three-day workshop on the burned hand; a three-week refresher course in physical rehabilitation; a one-week institute on supervision or sensory integration. Many opportunities are available throughout the country; in fact, the main difficulty is selecting those workshops that will be most helpful at any given time. Some employers will defray the costs of one or more educational workshops per year in the interest of keeping an up-to-date treatment program, but sometimes the therapist must underwrite this expense personally.

Graduate education leads to advanced degrees in selected fields of study. There are a number of postprofessional occupational therapy programs terminating in a master's degree and several doctoral programs. (See Appendix C at the back of this book for a complete listing of programs.) In addition, many occupational therapists seek advanced degrees in one of the foundation disciplines, such as biological sciences, behavioral sciences, human development, anthropology, social work, education, and guidance. These fields of study are all valuable for the therapist.

FINANCIAL AID AND COSTS

Educational costs have risen over the years, and there is a great difference in expense between tax-supported institutions (state, county, city) and privately endowed colleges. You are urged to contact the college of your choice for current information about its tuition and fees, living expenses, cost of books, and clinical fieldwork expenses.

The majority of students need to rely on financial aid packages that may include parents' contributions, personal savings, work-study programs, educational loans, and scholarships. A student's need for financial aid is, in the simplest terms, the difference between anticipated expenses and financial resources. The determination of need will be based upon analysis of information provided by the student and/or family. It is assumed that parents of dependent children ordinarily have an obligation to contribute to educational costs from discretionary income. For families below a moderate income level, little or no family contribution can be expected, and the students will need to secure the necessary funds.

A student is considered self-supporting if he or she is an older adult who has been financially independent for some time, or is not claimed as a dependent by her or his parents during a specified period preceding the determination of financial status.

If you are in need of financial assistance, you should look first to the possibilities of loans or scholarships from agencies in your community: your bank, church, service organizations, and other local foundations. Following acceptance into the occupational therapy program of your choice, contact the financial aid officer of that institution about the sources available through the college or university. Your occupational therapy program office also may have information about the numerous hospitals or other employers that support students by paying tuition for one or two years in return for a reasonable employment commitment (usually one to two years) as a full-salaried employee upon graduation.

Sign-on bonuses, often of several thousand dollars, are given by many employers. These are not typically given to students who have received tuition assistance from the same institution, or to those who obtained the position through the services of a recruiter (since the institution must pay the recruiter for finding the therapist).

There are sources of financial aid available to you beyond your own community. The suggestions offered here are merely a starting point; a trip to your public or school library should turn up additional sources of assistance.

Federal aid is available in the form of grants and loans. Grants are outright gifts of money to help you finance your education. Your demonstrated needs plus the type of school you are attending will determine the amount of the grant.

As you no doubt expected, federal loans must eventually be repaid by the student. But the terms of repayment are very generous. You pay nothing on the loan while you are enrolled in a program. Repayment begins after you leave school, and you have up to ten years to pay off the loan at a reasonable rate of interest.

Additionally, most states have grant and scholarship funds available to their residents. Both forms of assistance are outright gifts, but scholarships are generally based on outstanding academic performance and may be renewable every year that you are in school.

Many state occupational therapy associations offer loans and scholarships to students from their states. Contact your local association for more information on these programs.

The American Occupational Therapy Foundation (AOTF) administers scholarship programs that provide financial assistance to undergraduate and graduate occupational therapy students based on need and scholastic ability. Preference is given to college juniors and seniors or to students completing occupational therapy assistant programs. The E.K. Wise loan program assists eligible students who have baccalaureate degrees and are enrolled in advanced standing or graduate entry-level professional occupational therapy curricula, or who are enrolled in postprofessional graduate curricula in occupational therapy. The American Occupational Therapy Association provides information about financial assistance.

CERTIFICATION AND LICENSURE

Following graduation from an accredited professional program for occupational therapists, the graduate is eligible to take the national certification examination administered twice yearly by the American Occupational Therapy Certification Board. Successful completion leads to inclusion in a published registry of qualified professionals and the right to use the letters OTR after one's name.

Following graduation from an approved assistant program, the assistant is eligible to take a certification examination also administered by the American Occupational Therapy Certification Board. Successful completion of the examination leads to inclusion on a list of certified occupational therapy assistants and the right to use, following one's name, the letters COTA.

In 1976, the first state licensure laws were enacted in Florida, New York, Ohio, and Georgia. Most other states have followed suit and have legislated their own requirements and provisions for occupational therapists and assistants working within their borders. States requiring an examination for admission to licensure have elected to accept the American Occupational Therapy Certification Board examination for that purpose. You will need to make further inquiry concerning regulatory requirements in the state in which you plan to practice.

PERSONAL ATTRIBUTES

In addition to meeting educational requirements, there are identifiable personal qualities that are important to all therapists.

First and foremost among these qualities is a liking for people, followed by an enjoyment in sharing oneself with others and an ease in establishing relationships. Occupational therapy is a people-oriented profession, involving a teaching/counseling relationship with patients or clients and a coordinating/sharing relationship with other professionals.

The therapist needs to be empathetic and perceptive to the patient's feelings at a given moment in order to determine how best to respond. The therapist must be tactful and patient in working with clients, thereby avoiding undue friction and misunderstandings. Patients are people in crisis who are worried and anxious and may understandably be short-tempered. Misunderstandings between professionals also can be energy draining and time consuming and usually result in less effective treatment. A sense of humor is a great asset in helping to counteract the tensions of the day.

Communication skills are very important to the therapist. A good observer and listener will understand many problems before they are stated. It is also important to write and speak clearly. The therapist is a teacher with patients, families, the public, and professional colleagues; it is therefore important to be able to explain lucidly what has to be done, why, and what results are expected.

The therapist must be prepared to write reports describing treatment programs, administrative functions, or clinical research. It may be necessary to write grant proposals in order to obtain funding for special projects.

The potential therapist needs a certain degree of manual dexterity in some areas of practice and enjoyment of some creative activities, such as the arts, crafts, music, drama, and dance. It is not necessary to be an expert in the creative arts, but a certain amount of familiarity with them is helpful. The basic interest of the occupational therapist should be that of the teacher/counselor who experiences pleasure in guiding others, rather than that of the creative artist whose pleasure comes from expert performance. Remember, the creativity of the therapist is centered in the patient, whereas the creativity of the artist is centered in the artistic product. Creativity helps in the many decisions and problem solving required in evaluating, treating, and interacting with patients, colleagues, and others.

A few experiences useful to the would-be occupational therapist are: participating in special interest groups, such as music, art, drama, or journalism clubs; helping to organize social groups in school; volunteering in local hospitals and settlement houses; and leadership activities in scouting, Sunday school, summer camps for normal or handicapped children, and community centers. Any work or travel experience is beneficial to the growth of the individual and helpful in understanding people with different interests and lifestyles.

Occupational therapy is an exacting profession, and it demands much of the student. Curricula can be very demanding, and good study skills, determination, and perseverance are essential. Students who must work during their education or who have heavy home responsibilities will need good time management skills. Foreign students must have mastery of the English language when attending school in the United States, as well as equivalent academic credentials.

The therapist must use analytical skills in identifying problems and creativity in finding solutions. This is true whether the problem involves finding the best method to treat a child, approaching a man who has just lost his sight, convincing administrators that another therapist should be employed, or setting up a research project. Patients and other personnel expect the therapist to function as a leader—a person who is well prepared to do the job, has self-confidence, uses good judgment, and is dependable and responsible. Occupational therapists should not only have the courage to express convictions but also the ability to listen to other points of view and change position when proven wrong.

Physical and Mental Requirements

The person who wants to help patients with physical or mental problems must be well-adjusted. You must understand yourself and your methods of responding to crises, frustration, and anxiety before you can understand and share the problems of others. If you are meeting personal crises of your own, not much energy is left to give support to a sixteen-year-old boy who has just lost the use of his legs for life.

Physical health is also important, for when other people are dependent on you it is necessary to keep to your schedule. In many situations, the therapist is required to do a great deal of walking through long institutional corridors and traveling from home to home, or on public transportation, many times carrying equipment. Frequently it is necessary to support patients physically and lift children. The therapist should ideally have acute senses of sight, hearing, and touch in order to make keen observations of the patients.

There are, however, occupational therapists with disabilities who function well in certain settings. If you yourself have a disability that creates a functional handicap, you will need help in evaluating whether or not occupational therapy is a feasible career goal for you. You should seek counsel from the school of your choice.

CHAPTER 5

NATIONAL PROFESSIONAL SOCIETY

THE AMERICAN OCCUPATIONAL
THERAPY ASSOCIATION, INC.

Established in 1917, the American Occupational Therapy Association is the national professional organization for those who teach and practice occupational therapy. The association promotes better understanding of the profession and safeguards its standards of education and practice. It sponsors research and maintains communication with the membership and allied professions. As of 1998, total membership in the United States was over 57,000, including occupational therapists, occupational therapy assistants, and occupational therapy students. Members reside in all fifty states, the District of Columbia, Puerto Rico, and in fifty-eight foreign countries.

The national headquarters, in Bethesda, Maryland, is a liaison between state and regional associations, provides a large variety of regular and special services to therapists, and maintains educational services for the benefit of students, teachers, colleges, universities, and student affiliation centers.

The American Occupational Therapy Certification Board (AOTCB) administers the national certification examination for professional-level qualification (OTR) and the proficiency examination for the assistant-level qualification (COTA). It also maintains the registry of the American Occupational Therapy Association, which includes the names of all registered occupational therapists in the United States and a list of all certified occupational therapy assistants.

The certification process for either an OTR or a COTA assures the public, physicians, hospitals, patients, and fellow therapists of the individual's professional qualification to practice. It is the final step in the process of indicating competence for entry-level practice. The association sets standards for occupational therapy practice and assists new members in developing skills for monitoring quality of care.

There is an annual American Occupational Therapy Association conference. This conference is held in various geographical regions of the United States from year to year. The conference brings together thousands of therapists to learn from presentations and exhibits and to share ideas. (See Appendix B for the address and phone number of the AOTA and other related professional associations.)

Goals

1. To provide opportunities for the expression of members' concerns, to anticipate emerging issues to facilitate decision making, and to expedite the translation of these decisions into actions.
2. To support the development of research and knowledge bases for the practice of occupational therapists and to promote the dissemination of such information.
3. To facilitate and support an educational system for occupational therapy that responds to current health needs and anticipates, plans for, and accommodates change.
4. To promote occupational therapy as a viable health profession.
5. To facilitate the formation of partnerships with consumers to promote optimum health conditions for the public.

Affiliations

There are approximately fifty-two AOTA regional and state affiliates. These are the local professional and regional organizations and carry the names of the states that they cover in their organizational charters. Each affiliate is represented in the representative assembly, which meets once a year at the national conference.

Membership Services

1. Subscription to the *American Journal of Occupation Therapy*, the official organ of the association.
2. *OT Week*, a weekly news and employment publication.
3. Eleven *Special Interest Section Newsletters*.
4. *Journal of Occupational Therapy Students*.
5. Annual AOTA Conference.
6. Loan materials relative to career education, films, and visual aids.
7. Assistance in the implementation of administrative and clinical practice.
8. Assistance in recruitment and publicity.
9. Assistance in establishing educational and clinical administration policies.
10. Resource and consultation service regarding practice and related matters.
11. Listing of publications available to members at discount rates.
12. Staff support in legal and legislative issues of importance to occupational therapy professionals.
13. Sponsorship of continuing educational institutes and workshops.
14. Assistance to educational programs of occupational therapy through special studies in curriculum and teaching methods.

15. Occupational therapy library in the AOTA National Office, which includes computerized search services for a small fee.
16. Access to an online computerized information system.
17. Employment benefit program, including computerized job bank, employment exchange, placement information, and direct mail service in addition to the weekly employment bulletin.
18. Recognition program to grant awards for outstanding professional contributions.
19. Development of technical professional manuals for the use of students and other personnel.
20. Financial benefits program offering scholarships, fellowships, student loans, and grants.
21. Visitations for accrediting occupational therapy programs.
22. Insurance benefits program.

Special Interest Sections

Members of The American Occupational Therapy Association may choose to belong to one or more special interest sections, each of which pertains to one area of occupational therapy practice. These include administration and management, developmental disabilities, education, gerontology, home and community health, mental health, physical disabilities, school systems, sensory integration, and technology and work programs. These groups, through their leadership and the contributions of members, promote knowledge and skill development in specialized areas of practice. This role is fulfilled through informative publications, research, and promotion of continuing education. Special interest section members also act as liaisons to several national committees and advise the national office staff and the president of the national association on practice-related issues and publications.

WORLD FEDERATION OF OCCUPATIONAL THERAPISTS

The World Federation of Occupational Therapists is made up of member organizations in the following locations:

Argentina	Korea
Australia	Latvia
Austria	Luxembourg
Belgium	Malaysia
Bermuda	Malta
Brazil	Mauritius
Canada	Mexico
Chile	Netherlands
China	New Zealand
Colombia	Nigeria
Cypress	Norway
Denmark	Pakistan
Finland	Philippines
France	Portugal
Germany	Singapore
Greece	South Africa
Hong Kong	Spain
Iceland	Sri Lanka
India	Sweden
Ireland	Switzerland
Israel	Uganda
Italy	United Kingdom
Japan	United States of America
Jordan	Venezuela
Kenya	Zimbabwe

Although these are the current member organizations, occupational therapists are located in many additional countries, some of which have educational programs for occupational therapists. Occupational therapists with an interest in overseas employment may obtain a packet of information from the World Federation of Occupational Therapists.

The objectives of the federation are:

1. To act as the official international organization for the promotion of occupational therapy; to hold international congresses.
2. To promote international cooperation among occupational therapy associations, among occupational therapists, and between them and other allied professional groups.
3. To maintain the ethics of the profession and to advance the practice and standards of occupational therapy.
4. To promote internationally recognized standards for education of occupational therapists.
5. To facilitate the international exchange and placement of therapists and students.
6. To facilitate the exchange of information and publications and to promote research.

CHAPTER 6

EARNINGS AND
FRINGE BENEFITS

Most occupational therapists work for an annual salary, although some work on an hourly or on a per diem (so much per day) basis. Therapists in private practice are in a special class; their earnings are more difficult to estimate. There are substantial variations in salary among occupational therapy personnel who perform similar functions. This seems to be due, in part, to the different pay scales existing in the various geographic regions of the United States. The cost of living also varies from place to place, so you should consider a job offer in the context of the cost of living in that area. In general, occupational therapists are on a salary level comparable to those other health care professionals with similar training.

The following tables give minimum and maximum salaries for therapists with a variety of backgrounds, working in different practices. Your salary would probably fall somewhere in the range between high and low salaries. These data were compiled from a salary survey conducted by The American Occupational Therapy Association and reflect salary estimates for 1997. Salaries for all positions will probably be higher by the time you read this.

SALARY LEVELS

Annual Professional Income

OTRs AND COTAs
(FULL-TIME EMPLOYED)

Work Setting	OTRs	COTAs
All Settings	$47,095*	$31,126*
Self-Employed	51,938	32,875
Non-Self-Employed	46,902	30,921
Location in State		
Urban	47,657	30,708
Suburban	47,261	31,403
Rural	45,641	31,157

*Mean income

Annual Professional Income by Primary Employment Setting

(FULL-TIME EMPLOYED)

Setting	OTRs	COTAs
Government owned	$44,662*	$27,479*
Private for-profit	50,154	33,255
Private nonprofit	45,666	29,714
College or University (Faculty)		
Professor	$70,000**	
Associate professor	52,605	
Assistant professor	50,858	
Instructor	47,000	
Lecturer	45,662	

*Mean income
**Twelve-month appointment (average).

Annual Professional Income by Years of Experience
(FULL-TIME EMPLOYED)

Years of Experience	OTRs	COTAs
0–5	$41,740*	$29,858*
6–10	47,060	31,522
11–15	50,697	35,476
16+	50,723	31,638

*Mean income

Annual Professional Income by Highest Educational Degree
(FULL-TIME EMPLOYED)

Highest Educational Degree Level	OTRs
Baccalaureate	$46,228*
Master's	47,799
Doctorate	66,543
Certificate	52,718

	COTAs
Associate	$31,126
Baccalaureate	30,703
Master's	—
Doctorate	—
Certificate	34,650

*Mean income

Hourly Wage by Employment Status
(NON-SELF-EMPLOYED)

Hourly Wage	OTRs	COTAs
Mean	$24.04	$16.21
Median	22.61	15.38

(SELF-EMPLOYED)

Hourly Wage	OTRs	COTAs
Mean	$30.83	$21.93
Median	27.93	17.88

Annual Professional Income by State
(FULL-TIME EMPLOYED)

	OTRs	COTAs
Total U.S.	$47,095*	$31,126*
Alabama	$50,703	36,225
Alaska	—**	—
Arizona	48,227	28,760
Arkansas	41,139	—
California	52,263	34,987
Colorado	42,552	28,331
Connecticut	43,999	—
Delaware	—	—
District of Columbia	—	—
Florida	51,511	37,674
Georgia	45,577	31,179
Hawaii	—	—
Idaho	—	—
Illinois	45,884	32,386
Indiana	52,543	39,507
Iowa	39,007	—
Kansas	41,317	29,833
Kentucky	54,864	—
Louisiana	50,411	—
Maine	45,516	30,200
Maryland	45,778	—
Massachusetts	44,485	30,505
Michigan	43,798	34,469
Minnesota	39,183	23,610
Mississippi	—	—
Missouri	52,080	36,125
Montana	—	—
Nebraska	39,560	—
Nevada	46,681	—

	OTRs	COTAs
New Hampshire	$40,551	—
New Jersey	53,619	28,420
New Mexico	41,429	—
New York	46,889	30,768
North Carolina	48,017	33,400
North Dakota	31,387	—
Ohio	45,396	31,062
Oklahoma	54,389	33,833
Oregon	38,159	—
Pennsylvania	47,734	30,224
Puerto Rico	—	—
Rhode Island	62,250	—
South Carolina	55,838	—
South Dakota	33,833	—
Tennessee	46,359	—
Texas	48,621	31,697
Utah	51,667	—
Vermont	—	—
Virginia	47,553	33,300
Washington	42,131	24,439
West Virginia	—	—
Wisconsin	41,623	24,120
Wyoming	42,213	23,939

*Mean income
**No figures available
Source of income projections: 1997, AOTA Member Data Survey. (Estimates from prorated data.)

Although annual salary represents a large portion of most therapists' total compensation, it is by no means the only factor to be considered in evaluating a job offer. The total dollar worth of the fringe benefit package that comes with the job offer must be calculated into the adjusted (after taxes) salary to determine total compensation.

FRINGE BENEFITS

When faced with choosing one position over another with a similar salary, benefits often make a great deal of difference. It is quite possible that five job offers with exactly the same salary would offer five different benefit packages, so it is important that you become familiar with the following typical benefits and learn how to weigh them one against another.

• *Salary review.* After accepting a position at a certain starting salary, when would you come up for a salary review? In six months? A year? Longer? Is there a set schedule of salary increments?

• *Vacation.* Are your vacations paid? How much vacation will you be eligible for after one year of service? After five years? Can some portion of your salaried vacation be taken before the end of the term, based on accrued time? Can vacation time be saved up over two or more years, or must it be taken when due?

• *Sick leave.* How many days of sick leave may you take in one year? Are they paid? What happens if you exceed this limit?

• *Authorized absences.* Are you allotted a certain number of personal days per year? How many? What about leaves of absence for pregnancy or professional development? Do you receive any portion of your salary during these absences?

• *Advancement.* Are there clearly defined criteria for professional advancement? What additional titles, duties, and responsibilities would be open to you after several years of service? Is there room to move up into more responsible positions within the organization? Given the proper credentials, could you move freely from the clinical realm into administration or education?

• *Continuing education.* Are there any provisions for partial or total reimbursement for additional course work through graduate courses or continuing education seminars? Are your expenses for attending meetings and conferences paid? Are annual dues and membership fees for professional associations paid?

• *Malpractice.* Are you covered by insurance in case of malpractice suits?

• *Retirement.* Is there a pension plan or some other retirement program that you can participate in? What must you contribute? What are the benefits?

• *Health insurance.* Are there programs available to pay for your own personal health care? How much must you contribute?

In addition to salary and fringe benefits, other considerations such as work schedule, geographic location, and compatability with personal circumstances also will play a part in your job evaluation.

CHAPTER 7

CLINICAL PRACTITIONER

In the previous chapters we have considered occupational therapy and its various functions in relation to the spectrum of professional services it renders, both on a one-to-one client basis and in its community responsibilities. Let us now discuss some of the *professional* roles of the therapist. Broadly speaking, these roles can be divided into three large areas of rendered services:

• Positions in the clinical field in which effort is directed toward patient or client treatment. These roles are at the staff and supervisory level.

• Positions in professional education that are concerned with curriculum, teaching, and program development at both the undergraduate and graduate levels.

• Positions of general administration that are found in both the educational and clinical arenas. These positions require accumulated experience for the coordination and planning of various responsibilities, such as student supervision, class scheduling, curriculum structure, supervision of staff and other personnel, budget management, and personnel policies. All administrative positions are involved in planning and directing the work of others.

Research may be conducted by occupational therapists in any of the above roles or in positions designated specifically for research activities. Research is important for many reasons, including proving the value of one treatment over another.

In this chapter we will consider only the job description of the clinical practitioner. Administration will be dealt with more specifically in Chapter 9. Occupational therapists evaluate the functional potential of their clients and design programs of treatment to restore or enhance function.

SPECIFIC CLINICAL POSITIONS

Director of an Occupational Therapy Department

This position involves program development, implementation of planning, policy making, and all of the procedural duties for the smooth functioning of the department. In addition, the director is responsible for all personnel within the department and for all educational programs. The director reports to the medical director of the department for medical concerns and to the director of the institution or agency for administrative matters.

Assistant Department Director

The assistant department director assists the director of the department in the organization, administration, and coordination of all of the occupational therapy units of the department. This position is usually found only in larger institutions having many separate treatment units.

Supervisor of an Occupational Therapy Unit

The supervisor of an occupational therapy unit, in an institution having several units, may have both administrative and supervisory duties. The supervisor is responsible for the supervision and work assignments of staff therapists, students, auxiliary personnel, volunteers, and assistants assigned to the unit. Depending on the size of the unit, the supervisor may administer patient treatment. This person reports to the director of the department.

Supervisor of Student Fieldwork

This position entails great responsibility and preferably should be a senior staff therapist (OTR) with experience in handling personnel and students. This administrator coordinates programs of field experience for occupational therapy students working in the department, supervising their work and keeping in close contact with the affiliating institution. Some clinical duties also may be assumed.

JOB LOCATIONS

Occupational therapy offers a wide choice of geographical settings in which to practice, in both national and international opportunities.

In addition, there is great diversity of choice in field of practice. Some of the areas and programs in which the therapist works are: general hospitals, psychiatric facilities, rehabilitation centers, senior citizen centers, public and private schools, camps for handicapped children, nursing homes, cerebral palsy centers, community health projects, home health agencies, day care for geriatric and psychiatric clients, and private practice,

The following table, provided by The American Occupational Therapy Association, Inc., gives some idea of the diversity of treatment categories in which occupational therapists and occupational therapy assistants provide service. As previously mentioned, therapists work with individuals in a number of other diagnostic categories beyond the major classifications listed below.

Most Frequent Health Problems of Patients/Clients

Physical Health Problems	OTRs %	COTAs %
Amputation	0.1	0.3
Arteriosclerosis	0.1	0.3
Arthritis/Collagen Disorder	0.9	1.0
Back Injury	3.4	3.0
Burns	0.4	0.1
Cancer (Neoplasms)	0.2	0.3
Cardiopulmonary Diseases	0.7	0.4
Cerebral Palsy	9.7	6.0
Congenital Anomalies	0.3	0.1
CVA/Hemiplegia	27.1	30.3
Developmental Delay	12.9	8.9
Diabetes	0.1	0.1
Feeding Disorders	0.3	0.0
Fracture	2.3	3.0
Hand Injury	9.5	3.2
Hearing Disability	0.1	0.3
HIV Infections, incl. AIDS	0.1	0.0
Kidney Disorder	0.0	0.0
Learning Disabilities	7.0	5.1
Neuro/Muscular Disorder (e.g. MD, MS)	0.6	0.6
Respiratory Disease	0.1	0.2
Spinal Cord Injury	1.2	1.2
Traumatic Brain Injury	4.2	3.9
Visual Disability	0.3	0.0
Well Population	0.2	0.5

(continued)

Mental Health Problems	OTRs %	COTAs %
Adjustment Disorders	0.8	1.2
Affective Disorders	3.7	2.5
Alcohol/Substance Use Disorders	0.8	1.5
Alzheimer's Disease	0.6	2.2
Anxiety Disorders	0.1	0.4
Eating Disorders	0.2	0.1
Mental Retardation	4.9	11.4
Organic Mental Disorders*	0.8	2.1
Personality Disorders	0.6	0.8
Schizophrenic Disorders	4.1	6.6
Other Psychotic Disorders	0.1	0.2
Other Mental Health Disorders	0.6	1.1
Other:	0.8	1.1
Total	100.0	100.0
Physical Disabilities Combined	83.4	72.0
Mental Health Combined	16.6	28.0

Note: Respondents indicated the three most frequent health problems of their patients. This table describes only the most frequent. Additional information showing all three responses is available.
*Including Dementias and Organic Brain Syndromes, excluding Alzheimer's.

THE CLINICAL THERAPIST

The clinician is a client-centered therapist treating patients or clients whose lives have been interrupted by physical injury, disease, developmental defects, aging, mental health problems, drug abuse, or other factors.

The clinical therapist is an active practitioner who works directly with patients. This can be on a one-to-one basis or in a group situation. Treatment in some cases takes place in the home. Home visitations are made in many cases, in conjunction with the visiting nurse or physical therapist, often working out of state social services or public health programs.

STAFF DUTIES

The major duties of a staff occupational therapist in a hospital may be considered in three broad dimensions:

1. Patient treatment: evaluation, goal setting, treatment, reporting
2. Departmental routines: scheduling, accountability, maintenance of equipment, ordering supplies, conducting inventories
3. Educational activities: supervising, orienting, advising, presenting service and continuing education programs

Each patient poses a different problem, for no two patients are exactly alike. One of the things that makes occupational therapy such an exciting profession is this diversity and variety.

Consider the following medical conditions with which you might be confronted: developmental or behavioral problems; psychiatric and emotional conditions; speech and auditory disorders; cerebrovascular accident (stroke); multiple sclerosis; head injuries; and spinal-cord injuries.

ENTRY-LEVEL POSITIONS

The first entry-level job in the field is usually a staff position under the supervision of a clinical supervisor. As job experiences and competencies are gained, the therapist usually progresses into positions of greater responsibility, such as student supervision and clinical teaching.

The time lapse before job promotion rests, of course, with the therapist, depending on his or her interest, motivation, and dedication. Ascending job responsibilities occur at about two- to four-year intervals. But job advancement may occur rapidly, based on ability. Occupational therapy is one of the fastest growing health professions, making employment and advancement opportunities excellent.

SCIENTIFIC KNOWLEDGE

The occupational therapist must have a good background of scientific knowledge concerning the normal and pathological structure and function of the human body.

Any interrupted pathways of the sensory-input or motor-output systems will, of course, result in impaired sensorimotor responses. The therapist is educated to be aware of symptoms indicating dysfunction. Such symptom pictures serve as the basis for preparing treatment programs incorporating purposeful activities and skill development for each patient. Learning about normal and abnormal psychological functioning and psychiatric dysfunction is also a necessary part of an occupational therapist's education. Such knowledge helps therapists understand the emotional accompaniments of both physical and psychological disorders.

PSYCHOLOGICAL ASPECTS OF APPROACH

Whether the therapist is working with patients or clients in fine motor skills through activities, in job-related skills such as typing, or in neuromuscular therapy, he or she works to improve functioning in physical or psychological daily living skills. The patient's recovery is the primary goal. The pleasure and sense of accomplishment derived from these activities is of great psychological benefit; the end product of the activity, if any, is secondary. For example, the process of making a craft item, if used in physical dysfunction therapy, is more important, by virtue of exercising and developing certain muscles, than the way the finished product looks. Along with physical improvement, it is important to watch for emotional progress in patients, since both physical and psychological well-being are important to occupational therapy. In a psychiatric facility, of course, the emotional aspect is of prime importance.

THERAPIST CONCERNS

Thus, whatever the condition that impedes the patient's ability to engage in and fully perform tasks of daily living, occupational therapy seeks to aid in the development of coping skills. Occupational therapy is a health profession whose primary focus is the enhancement of adaptive skills and performance capacity. Therapists are concerned with factors that are barriers to the individual's capacity to function, either mentally or physically.

The therapist must understand the patient's or client's mental attitudes, motivating factors, and readiness for individual or group participation. Careful records are kept relative to the patient's progress from admittance to discharge. This is for the protection of both the patient or client and the therapist. In addition, careful records ensure continuity and quality of care in the event of a change in therapists or re-admission.

EVALUATION TECHNIQUES

The clinician must have a sound knowledge of human development and the nervous system, together with an understanding of sensorimotor integration, in order to interpret evaluation findings.

The techniques of administering various tests used for evaluation are taught to the student in occupational therapy academic programs. Practice in evaluation techniques is obtained in the clinical fieldwork portion of the study program.

A few examples of some areas in which occupational therapists carry out evaluations should give the reader a basic understanding of types of evaluations clinicians must perform before beginning treatment. Within each of these areas, and in others not mentioned, there may be many specific tests from which to choose. In certain instances, therapists must devise a test to elicit the information needed to plan treatment. Although the therapist must record results by notation or on checklists or forms, the majority of tests do not involve paper and pencil responses by the patient or client. Rather, the therapist more often asks the subject to perform a task incorporating the behavior being noted or observes the individual in a naturalistic or uncontrived setting that is likely to elicit the physical, emotional, social, or cognitive-based responses pertinent to therapy. Whenever possible (depending on mental and physical condition, age, etc.), results of the evaluation are discussed with the patient or client and he or she is involved in setting goals for treatment.

• *Developmental tests* are used to assess a child's gross motor, fine motor, adaptive, language, and personal-social skills. Various performance items are observed and recorded on forms that, when scored, indicate the developmental level of the child in each of the above skill areas. These tests also are helpful at times in assessing older developmentally delayed persons. When delays are found in one or more areas, therapy is initiated to provide developmental stimulation. Children who are hospitalized for long periods of time are likely to fall behind others in their age group unless developmentally appropriate activities are provided during hospitalization. Results of the evaluation may also be used to counsel parents on appropriate methods of enhancing development.

There are two basic types of *daily living skills.* Physical daily living skills procedures evaluate the patient's ability to walk, sit, dress, accomplish self-feeding, care for personal hygiene, use the telephone, and perform other daily self-help tasks. Psychological/ emotional daily living skills refer to performance in developing personal self-concept or self-identity, situational coping, and community or societal involvement.

A treatment program then will be planned to help the patient or client perform the activities that he or she needs and is able to do. This may be accomplished by muscle-strengthening through exercise, body positioning, performance practice, or by using adapted equipment.

Occupational therapists are well equipped to design and make adapted devices or splints for patients to aid them in the activities of daily living. Many devices are commercially available, but custom-made devices may be necessary.

• *The homemaker evaluation* tries to determine how well a patient can use the necessary equipment to care for a home. For example, how well is a wheelchair-bound patient able to use the stove, sink, and other kitchen equipment? Are cabinets at a level where various homemaker tools can be reached? Are there modifications that can be made on the wheelchair, or in the room, that would enable the patient to prepare a meal in the kitchen? Are there bathroom modifications, such as handrails on the tub, that can be made? Do the patient's clothes have zippers and easy snaps that will facilitate getting dressed?

• *The sensorimotor evaluation* includes assessment of the client's ability to receive stimuli through the senses of sight, hearing, smell, taste, touch, equilibrium, and of his or her ability to react to them. This also implies the neurological function of interpreting the stimuli.

Study of sensory integration by many occupational therapists has resulted in the development of measurement tools, based upon scientific data, with which therapists can more accurately assess cognitive, perceptual, motor, and behavioral problems. These tests are of use to the therapist in planning treatment procedures.

Until recently there had been few scientific methods of measurement in the cognitive-perceptual field. It was not understood why Johnny could not interpret what he saw, felt, read, or heard, or why his sense of balance was impaired. Basic scientific evaluations now are available that point the way toward a better understanding of these and other problems related to cognitive-perceptual motor processes.

Treatment is based on the selection of activities that will give practice in performing the underdeveloped function. Substitute functions also may be developed and tasks adapted by positioning of the patient and/or the use of equipment.

• *Range of motion* is a measurement of the amount of motion present at any given joint. Distance between a position of extension (straight) and a position of flexion (bent), or other motions, is measured.

If joints are stiff and show a limited range of motion, activities are selected that will exercise these joints. Conservation of diseased joints also may be a goal.

• *Testing of muscle strength* evaluates the status of individual muscles or muscle groups—for instance, whether the muscles of the wrist are strong enough to flex and extend that joint. Progressive resistive exercises are used in treatment directed toward strengthening specific muscle groups. The goal is to improve functional ability by overcoming weakness or to help the client or patient discover alternative ways to increase independence.

Activities requiring *coordination and dexterity* are used to determine how well certain groups of muscles work together to produce smooth, coordinated action. Can a child get a spoon to the mouth, or is assistance needed? Coordination and dexterity measure the quickness and accuracy of a patient's ability to perform certain functional tasks.

As must be obvious to the reader, we have been examining very special areas of function that are closely interrelated and overlapping. It therefore follows that treatment programs are equally interrelated.

Neurodevelopmental approaches to treatment are based on developmental patterns controlled by the nervous system. Neurophysiological approaches are based on the interplay between the sensory and motor functions of the nervous system. There are many highly specialized techniques in use today to assist patients with muscle coordination and sensory problems.

• *Vocational evaluation* assesses the client's cognitive and physical abilities; work skills, habits, and interests; social adjustment; and potential employability. Partial simulation of work activities may be used, The results of these evaluations are usually made available to a vocational counselor, who may arrange for job training as indicated.

• *Body image evaluations* determine the patient's ability for body visualization, such as locating various parts of the body relative to positioning. Following a cerebrovascular accident (stroke) the patient may have difficulty in determining his or her body position and may sustain a changed body concept because of paralysis and loss of function on one side of the body.

• *Personality and object relations* play an important part in adjusting to daily routines of living. Therapists analyze the individual's effort and ability to carry out daily life skills in a manner that provides personal satisfaction and a productive role of satisfying living. Evaluation procedures are used to make a basic assessment of the client. Some of the personality concepts evaluated include self-concept, concept of others, communication skills and personal conflicts. These and other areas of function are evaluated to reach a basic personality assessment of the patient or client and to aid the occupational therapist in the treatment of various emotional problems.

Object relations concerns the relationship behavior of the client with animate and inanimate things in his or her environment. This would include people, pets, plants, and inanimate objects such as toys and furniture.

The identification of problems that are preventing the patient from developing satisfactory relationships in his or her environment is the first step to helping overcome them. Treatment may be planned as an individual activity with the therapist or as a group activity with peers depending upon the unique problems presented.

Thus the therapist is constantly faced with a variety of treatment situations of a physical or psychological nature. These situations extend all the way from the infant to the senior citizen. The occupational therapist plays an important part in health care for disabled and ill persons.

RESULTS DOCUMENTATION

The careful recording of all evaluation and treatment procedures used for any given patient or client is a requisite to quality care. Evaluation results and interpretation help occupational therapists to plan treatment and the health care team members to make decisions regarding further treatment or outside placement. Results also aid family members in planning for care, making financial arrangements, and so forth. Not only is the therapist responsible for sharing information orally with other concerned members of the service community, but he or she also must take care in keeping the client's record. The total treatment process, therefore, encompasses the processes of evaluation, goal setting, program development, program implementation, and documentation of results.

CHAPTER 8

WORK ENVIRONMENTS

Five broad categories of agencies employ occupational therapists. The areas are: federal, state, municipal, and nonprofit and for-profit. The services of these health delivery centers overlap in some instances, but generally speaking these categories cover the broad spectrum of positions where one finds therapists at work. Other areas of employment, such as private practice, hospice, and foreign service employment, also will be discussed in this chapter.

FEDERAL AGENCIES

Under federal agencies employing occupational therapists come the armed forces, which include the United States Army, Navy, and Air Force, with their medical specialist corps and sections. The Department of Veterans Affairs caters to the needs of disabled veterans. The U.S. Public Health Service (USPHS) is the principal health agency of the federal government. Its main objective is to protect and advance the health of American citizens. Because of their expertise and knowledge of the health care system, some occupational therapists have assumed higher-level health-related positions in the federal government.

• *The Department of Veterans Affairs Medical Centers* are under the civil service system and number over 170 hospitals in the United States, the District of Columbia, and Puerto Rico. They provide ongoing care with medical, surgical, rehabilitation, and psychiatric services for military veterans.

Appointments for occupational therapists are made through the Civil Service system. Applicants must be United States citizens in good health and graduates of approved programs in occupational therapy. Both men and women are accepted.

• *The U.S. Army.* Applicants for an occupational therapy army career must hold a minimum of a bachelor's degree from an approved program in occupational therapy.

The army's medical specialist corps, of which occupational therapy is a part, offers many opportunities to promote professional growth. As an officer and member of the army medical team, the applicant may qualify to attend several educational programs, such as the advanced officer's course or army hospital courses. Assignments in other countries are sometimes given. For information write to the Surgeon General, HQUDASGPE, PDO: Room 7-B054, Forrestal Building, Washington, DC 20314.

• *The U.S. Navy.* Applicants for navy service must be fully qualified occupational therapists. This includes a bachelor's degree from an accredited college or university and certification after completing an approved course in occupational therapy. They must be citizens of the United States, physically and professionally qualified, and at least eighteen years of age at the time of appointment.

A navy occupational therapist is a part of the multidisciplinary rehabilitation team in the navy medical department. The occupational therapist plans and supervises treatment programs for patients with a wide range of physical and emotional dysfunctions. As a member of the navy medical service corps, the therapist will serve in naval hospitals throughout the United States. For more information write to the Chief, Bureau of Medicine and Surgery, Department of the Navy, Washington, DC 20372.

• *The U.S. Air Force.* The minimum educational requirements for USAF positions are a bachelor's degree and the completion of an approved course in an occupational therapy school. If accepted, assignments are made to air force medical centers and regional hospitals.

The air force uses the health care team concept of integrating the biomedical sciences into a worldwide system. Each health care discipline is centered around medical complexes, which are organized for clinical seminars and teaching. Each center is affiliated with a medical school program of continuing education, which is designed to keep officers abreast of current medical, psychological, and biological specializations.

Thus, the air force occupational therapist is exposed to and works with many kinds of physical and mental dysfunctions. Applicants must be at least eighteen years of age. Contact the Associate Chief of the B.S.C. for Occupational Therapy, Department of the Air Force, Wilford Hall, USAF Medical Center, Lackland AFB, TX 78236 for additional information.

• *The U.S. Public Health Service.* As stated before, the USPHS is the principal health agency of the federal government. Its main objective is to advance the health of citizens and to do basic health research in designated areas of environmental medicine.

The occupational therapist will find many challenging and interesting positions in this service. Chronic diseases are studied, coordination of community services is evaluated, and new treatments for stroke, mental illness, heart disease, and other conditions are constantly tested and refined. The opportunity for the therapist in public health is a unique and meaningful one, particularly for those with an inquiring mind.

Initially the staff therapist receives a staff or outpatient assignment, progressing to a supervisory level. Certain civil service and agency requirements must, of course, be met. Some therapists work in the Peace Corps, accepting assignments in foreign countries after extensive orientation to the culture and needs of the host country. Write to the USPHS at 5600 Fishers Lane, Rockville, MD 20857 for further information.

STATE AGENCIES

Each state has an agency for services to the physically and mentally handicapped. Under governmental jurisdictions, care has been extended to victims of cerebral palsy, birth defects, congenital heart defects, and other disabling diseases.

The objective of state services for children with special needs is to search out all children from birth on with potentially handicapping conditions. A health team of the various disciplines, of which occupational therapy is one, works to restore as much function and social organization as possible to the client. Most of the staff therapists in these programs give direct patient care, teach and counsel parents, demonstrate care and use of braces and artificial limbs, and plan activities to restore functions. The state consultant of such a program educates the staff, evaluates their performance, and makes proper reports to the state authorities. These consultants also are active in community affairs, addressing various groups and explaining the service programs to them.

In addition, occupational therapists are employed in state institutions designed to provide for the needs of the mentally ill and developmentally disabled.

MUNICIPAL DEPARTMENTS

Large general hospitals are usually found in cities and have well-equipped occupational therapy departments and staffs. Almost all medical schools are attached to general hospitals, which are usually teaching hospitals for professional students of all disciplines. All types of medical disabilities are found in this environment, together with many departments, such as orthopedic, neurological, dermatological, ophthalmological, psychiatric, and pediatric. Special clinics for patients with cerebral palsy, spina bifida, diabetes mellitus, and other conditions may exist in these hospitals.

Public schools employ many therapists to work with children having physical disabilities, learning disabilities, emotional problems, or various developmental delays.

NONPROFIT AND FOR-PROFIT AGENCIES

Nonprofit agencies are supported by private funds and endowments. Two of the largest and best-known agencies in this area are the United Cerebral Palsy Association, Inc., and the National Easter Seal Society. These agencies have a great many state affiliates that are directly involved in the delivery of health services. Nonprofit agencies offer many different types of positions in occupational therapy. Persons interested in this kind of professional work should apply directly to the affiliate organization in their respective states. For-profit agencies also employ occupational therapists in similar positions.

REHABILITATION CENTERS

There are many rehabilitation centers in the United States due to favorable federal legislation and the consistent and unflagging work of the national and local nonprofit agencies involved. Rehabilitation units are found in for-profit facilities as well.

Rehabilitation, as such, is not just treatment for one condition. It concerns all medical services and allied health personnel. The occupational therapist, the physical therapist, the physician, the nurse, the social worker, and other closely allied professional persons such as the psychologist, the teacher, and the vocational counselor all participate in the rehabilitation program. The patient's family members also play an important role in this process.

The philosophy of rehabilitation includes all the medical, psychosocial, and vocational aspects of the client. It means that the goals of treatment are directed toward as complete a restoration of physical function and social living as it is possible for the client to achieve.

Rehabilitation procedures are in many cases under the jurisdiction of a physiatrist–a medical specialist in the treatment of rehabilitation medicine. However, the physiatrist is also aware of the other medical and social components present in the total rehabilitation of a client and will make referrals to other professionals as indicated.

These other professional services may well come from other community facilities and medical sources. They may be in nearby hospitals, outpatient clinics, or through home visitation by public health or private home health personnel. They may, if needed, come from delivery of health services in the public school system, an area in which many occupational therapists now practice.

Some of the rehabilitation services in a community that may be within a rehabilitation center are as follows:

- services of medical specialists;
- social casework to assist client and family;
- physical therapy services;
- occupational therapy services for evaluation in physical, psychosocial, and vocational areas, and treatment as necessary;
- speech and hearing therapy;
- special education for the handicapped;
- psychological and counseling services;

- vocational counseling with reference to employment;
- residential clubs to adjust to outside living;
- halfway houses, which aid in the readjustment of the psychiatric client returning to the community;
- sheltered workshops and remunerative centers;
- independent living centers; and
- adult day care.

INDUSTRIAL CLINICS

Many large insurance companies maintain their own rehabilitation centers, where their clients are sent for treatment and where their progress can be watched at close hand. The Liberty Mutual Company of Boston has been a pioneer in this field. Hand injuries, multiple fractures, sprains, strains, dislocations, crush injuries, amputations, and ruptured discs and other back injuries are high frequency disabilities found in many of the larger cities. This type of industrial occupational therapy covers a broad spectrum and offers well-paid and interesting positions for the therapist. Individual therapists also have set up their own private clinics for industry-related disabilities.

PRIVATE PRACTICE

Increasing numbers of occupational therapists are entering the rapidly expanding area of private practice. As more insurance companies provide financial coverage for occupational therapists, private practice therapists are encouraged to venture into this growing area of practice, due to the helpful third-party involvement in the payment of the fees that cover patient treatment. Many of these therapists contract with agencies, hospitals, and physicians to provide services.

The therapist contemplating private practice should have at least three to six years of experience in a clinical specialty, a sound knowledge of business practice, and a thorough knowledge of the national, state, and local laws governing such practice. Legal and ethical procedures must be of prime concern to independent therapists in private practice, since they do not have the support and guidance of an institution in legal matters.

The therapist should have a wide acquaintance with physicians and organizations, both in medical facilities and in rehabilitation as well as other health-related centers. Such information should be procured in advance of soliciting clients and going into private practice. Informal meetings with key local health care personnel are advised, to ascertain whether the community can support a private practice.

Adequate insurance coverage is necessary for all parties concerned, to cover any incidents that might occur during treatment. Contact The American Occupational Therapy Association for insurance details.

The equipment necessary for private case–handling is expensive and extensive and must be paid for by the therapist running the private clinic. Maintenance expenses, such as rent, heat, light, telephone, and other incidentals also must be calculated to give a complete expense estimate.

HOSPICES

A changed attitude concerning the care of the dying is a very prominent feature of today's health care system. In the past, patients sometimes approached death without much care or understanding.

Hospices are organized for just the opposite reason: to teach the patient to learn to live with his or her terminal condition and to meet death with a degree of peace of mind. Patients in a hospice are treated as normally as possible. There are beauty salons, recreational activities, and discussion groups. Death is a subject that is discussed openly. Hospices are run on a family basis, providing understanding and kindness. Family interaction and participation is encouraged.

But why mention hospices in connection with occupational therapists? Therapists receive excellent basic training in psychosocial services, and are thus well equipped to deal with terminal illness and the care required. Dying is a fact of life—one that the therapist is sure to encounter. Psychological support for terminally ill patients is an important service that occupational therapists are well qualified to provide.

Hospice care combines three concerns:

1. *Pain control.* It is a fundamental belief of the hospice that pain need not be a problem and that its adequate control should consist of the right medicinal dosage at the right time.

2. *Thoughtful personal treatment.* Hospice staff members treat the patient as a whole person. Drugs are used to relieve pain, not to prolong life. It is important in hospice care to give the patients as much control over their lives as they are able to manage.

3. *Family support.* Members of the family are welcome at any time of the day or night and are urged to stay with patients if they wish.

OVERSEAS ASSIGNMENTS

Some occupational therapists secure foreign service employment through the Peace Corps, the World Federation of Occupational Therapists (discussed in Chapter 5), or other groups. Not everyone will want to practice this profession abroad, but the following pointers should be helpful to those who find this idea attractive.

These assignments are exciting, but one must remember that they were not set up for the opportunists who would use a job as a stepping-stone to a free world tour!

When accepting a foreign assignment, it is a good idea to read as much as you can about the country in which you plan to work. Learn as much as possible relative to the social customs, economic conditions, religion, history, and geography of the country, and try to fit into its pattern of living. It will differ from what you are accustomed to, and you must avoid the temptation to "reform" nationals in other countries to your way of life. The well-accepted therapist overseas is the one who tries to live as much as possible as the people in the visited areas live and does not demand preferential accommodations or other special treatment.

No matter what country you select, or who is sponsoring you, you will need certain official papers: a passport, visas, health certificate, driver's license, and a work permit.

You also will need to be immunized against diseases such as typhoid, typhus, or other diseases prevalent in the area where you will serve.

CHAPTER 9

ADMINISTRATION

To function effectively as an occupational therapist, you must understand the responsibilities and concerns of your supervisors, as well as the needs of your patients or clients. An understanding of the administrative structure of your department will be useful even to those who intend to serve in a strictly clinical capacity. This chapter will use the example of a hospital occupational therapy department to discuss administration, although many therapists are employed in wide-ranging types of administrative positions in nonhospital settings.

DUTIES OF AN ADMINISTRATOR

Although many therapists become administrators beyond the department level, this section will focus on the administration of occupational therapy departments. Departments of occupational therapy are organized and administered in accordance with the policies of the employing agency. These policies should be well understood by all personnel. The usual routine duties connected with the administration of a clinical department include:

1. direction and supervision of all personnel in the occupational therapy department;
2. maintenance of supplies and equipment;

3. maintenance of departmental records;
4. responsibility for periodic reports of departmental activities;
5. promotion of community relations;
6. program development;
7. marketing of available services; and
8. recruiting and hiring personnel.

Employment

The employment of personnel varies considerably, depending on the employment policies of the facility. In many instances, the responsibility of finding, interviewing, and hiring qualified staff members lies with the department director. In other instances, all employment is done through a central personnel office, and the therapist is only asked to conduct an interview, review the records of the individual in question, and accept or reject the applicant.

Orientation

All personnel assigned to a department must be familiarized with the regulations and policies of the institution and those of the department itself. They must clearly understand their duties and responsibilities and what the facility expects of them. They must understand the organizational system of the institution and the lines of authority. For example, the staff therapist is directly responsible to the director of the department, while students or aides are responsible to the staff therapist designated to supervise students. Each occupational therapy department should have its own set of personnel policies.

Treatment Schedules

The staff therapist also must schedule the treatment of patients, and the supervisor must see that the patient load is equitably divided among staff members. The therapist must know when a patient will be available for treatment, schedule the patient at available times, and check to be sure that the patient reports at the scheduled time.

Conferences

All departments, whether large or small, should arrange periodic conferences for all personnel. This is the director's responsibility. Some departments have conferences for fifteen minutes or so every morning, others once a week at a regularly scheduled time, and others meet only once a month. Usually, these conferences include departmental policy changes, problems of expansion and supply, and specific patient problems. In this way, all personnel are promptly notified of any new developments, and all have responsibility for contributing to the planning of the group.

A departmental director or supervisor also should arrange to have individual supervisory conferences periodically with all personnel assigned to him or her. These conferences are used to evaluate work performance, to discuss program development in each therapist's specialty area, and to hear concerns of personnel. The director should always be available to give help and guidance as needed.

Morale

Maintaining good morale and having solid working relationships with your staff are important. The wise therapist will be supportive of *all* staff members, affording equal privileges and opportunities for and showing favoritism to none. A policy of this kind will avoid the occasion for petty jealousies and grudges between staff members.

Supplies and Equipment Maintenance

The duties of the therapist relative to the maintenance of supplies and equipment include ordering or purchasing, maintaining inventories, and seeing to the care and repair of equipment. Equipment refers to nonexpendable items that require replacement only after hard use or loss.

Sliding Inventory

In order to know what supplies are on hand and when it is necessary to reorder, a carefully maintained stock sliding inventory must be kept. Likewise, an inventory of nonexpendable equipment is necessary, because the therapist is responsible to the institution for all equipment consigned for the department's use and must report all lost or worn-out items.

Monthly Reports

The therapist usually needs to submit a monthly report or summary of all activities within the department. Departmental records form the basis for such a report: patient treatment statistics; personnel who have been employed or who have resigned; new procedures that have been instituted during the period; any changes that have taken place; special events that have been planned for patients (picnics, outings, parties, holiday events); visitors to the department; newly acquired equipment; and educational activities and seminars. Productivity reporting and quality assurance activities help ensure effective treatment at reasonable cost. This information is usually incorporated into an annual report that is submitted to the director, who in turn submits a master annual report. An annual budget also is submitted by the director of occupational therapy, in both academic and clinical situations, to the institution.

Medical Charts

The therapist has access to the patient's medical chart. This is privileged information and should not be discussed with the patient or others. If the patient or family desire information about the medical record, they should ask the physician directly.

Ward Rounds

In addition, the therapist may spend a part of each day accompanying physicians on ward rounds or in clinical visitations. At this time, new patients are examined and treatments are prescribed. Progress is noted in patients who have been under treatment. Physicians also may advise necessary changes in treatment procedures.

Staff Conferences

Staff conferences of various kinds are usually held in institutions and agencies, and perhaps the most helpful ones to the therapist are those that are patient-centered. All members of the staff meet to discuss the problems of specific patients. Each member reports the progress made. Here we see the combined thinking of many specialists, pooling their efforts to bring the greatest benefit to the patient. Problems are discussed, treatment emphases are changed, or the group may decide that maximum benefit has been derived.

Multidisciplinary Approach to Treatment

Another consideration in the planning of a treatment program is the correlation of occupational therapy with other therapies being administered. Staff conferences, discussed above, are an important means of correlation.

The therapist should know not only which other departments are treating the patient, but also what goals they are working toward, when treatments are scheduled, and the length of each daily treatment. For example, if a patient is receiving treatment in physical therapy for restoration of function in a stiff elbow joint, the occupational therapist should know what exercises are being given and how they are being done. The same motion can then be carried over into the occupational therapy treatment.

Evaluation of Treatment

The therapist must watch for signs of fatigue or for any contraindications to treatment. The therapist also observes signs of change in the physical or mental attitudes, for these may indicate a need for changes in treatment.

The therapist evaluates the treatment according to changes in the patient's condition. This may mean longer or shorter work periods, increasing or decreasing the physical demands of the work and the amount of coordination required, and increasing concentration, mental effort, and responsibility. If, however, there appear to be indications for a change of total treatment goals, then the therapist must confer with the physician and other team members and proceed in accordance with revised goals. Therapists may conduct research to investigate results of individual or group patient treatment, which provides valuable information relative to quality of patient care.

COMMUNITY RELATIONS

Community relations is an important part of the work of the therapist. It is essential that the therapist establish and maintain a good working relationship with all patients and personnel of the agency. A satisfactory and congenial relationship requires thought and continuing action. It is accomplished by friendliness, courtesy, respect, and consideration for others and for their rights.

Good community relations must be maintained not only with the institutional "family," so to speak, but also with all visitors to the institution with whom the therapist comes into contact. The therapist becomes a host to any visitors to the clinic and must explain to them as clearly as possible the functions of the profession. Building and maintaining good public relations is a duty not only within the walls of the institution, but also in all contacts with the community at large. The therapist always must represent not only herself or himself but also serve the profession and the employing facility. The goodwill created reflects upon all three.

COMMUNITY SERVICES

The last point to be considered under departmental administration is that of community resources. The community in which the department is located becomes a potential source of diversified help to the therapist and the patients. It is important to acquire as wide a knowledge of these resources as possible. Among the first things that a therapist should learn about are the various sources within the community that can be used for the benefit of the patient. What other agencies, such as sheltered workshops, homebound services, rehabilitation centers, vocational rehabilitation, employment services, senior citizen groups, and youth training resources, are available to the patient?

If patients are served who need vocational rehabilitation, the therapist should have knowledge of the job opportunities within the community. What are the industries of the community? What are the jobs in these industries that might be open to patients? How many people are already trained to do these jobs? For example, it would be foolish to encourage a patient toward an interest in radio and television repair if there are already too many such repair workers for the community to support.

Aside from the many sources that may be tapped for the direct benefit of the patient, there are other sources that may broaden the scope of the occupational therapy program and, therefore, bring indirect help to the patient. The community itself is the source for volunteer help. If the therapist wants volunteer help in the department, an assessment must be made to determine if the community has people who are interested in volunteering. The therapist should know, too, if the organizational machinery is already set up for the recruitment and training of volunteers, or if establishment of a program is necessary.

The public library is another valuable source of aid, as is the art museum, if one is available. Both have resource materials that may be borrowed and staff who are in a position to advise and help the therapist.

PROFESSIONAL PROMOTION

Every graduate therapist is charged with the responsibility of utilizing every possible opportunity to interpret clearly and correctly the functions of the profession. As is evident to the reader, this is a growing and changing profession that must be constantly interpreted to members of the medical profession and to the lay public alike. Interpretation may be done verbally during casual conversations, and by lectures, demonstrations, written articles, or films.

Within the institution where the therapist is employed, he or she should accept invitations to discuss the profession of occupational therapy with various groups. New staff physicians should be invited to visit the occupational therapy department during treatment periods so that the proper use of the department may be explained and demonstrated. New interns and residents and house doctors should be contacted and introduced to the department as soon as possible after their arrival. The therapist will have frequent opportunity to give orientation lectures to nurses, attendants, and other personnel.

The therapist will be invited to lecture to various community groups regarding the purposes of the profession and the educational requirements to enter it. As mentioned previously, many of these groups will visit the institution and tour the department.

EDUCATIONAL DUTIES

The actual educational duties of the administrative therapist will depend to a large extent upon whether he or she is employed in a teaching hospital or whether the department of occupational therapy is affiliated, for training purposes, with an accredited educational program in occupational therapy (see Chapter 10 for additional information on teaching positions).

Clinical Affiliations/Fieldwork

If the department is a clinical education center for occupational therapy students, the clinical teaching program will be arranged for varying lengths of time for each disability area designated, depending upon arrangements made with the school. In any event, the students are there for a set period of time. Early in their educational program students may merely observe or perform simple duties in line with their current level of skills. The final level of fieldwork, sometimes called an internship or affiliation, requires the baccalaureate student to spend six months, full-time, in one or more settings, gaining a minimum of three months' experience in physical dysfunction and three months in psychosocial dysfunction under supervision. The responsibilities of the supervising therapist include: planning the students' work schedule; arranging for attendance at clinics, staff meetings, and any special lectures or demonstrations; organizing field trips to nearby institutions and community agencies; teaching treatment procedures; and supervising and guiding the student as treatment is given.

Volunteers

Another group that may add to the educational responsibilities of the therapist are volunteers. If the institution approves the use of volunteers in the occupational therapy department, and no training facilities have been set up in the community, the therapist will have to organize a training course. Volunteers must receive instruction regarding the policies of the agency and department. They must know general precautions to be observed if they are to have direct patient contact. Finally, the therapist must teach them the skills and activities in which their aid is needed. The therapist has full responsibility for volunteers as they work in the clinical settings, with responsibility for their errors as well as for their services.

CHAPTER 10

TEACHING

THE ART AND SCIENCE OF EDUCATION

A purveyor of knowledge, an attentive listener, and a sympathetic counselor—these are the attributes of a good teacher. Teaching in an academic program that prepares occupational therapists is not an easy job. The demands are constant, and you must be a dedicated person with a genuine desire to teach and the enthusiasm to impart knowledge to students. The ability to stimulate students to think for themselves, to be problem solvers, and to make good value judgments is a rare quality.

Teaching is an art, but scientific findings can be of practical value in helping the teacher to understand students better and to modify personal attitudes and behaviors based on more astute observations. Research findings may provide insight into better ways of presenting material.

Effective teaching takes a great deal of preparation. For each hour of teaching, two or three hours must be spent in routine preparation procedures. This involves, among other things, preparing course objectives and schedules; writing and giving examinations; grading papers; and, one of the most rewarding aspects of teaching, student conferences, wherein one gains insight to students' thinking. Occupational therapy faculty members in most institutions of higher learning are expected to conduct research and to publish in their areas of expertise. Those are common requirements for promotion and tenure in colleges and universities.

This excursion into the philosophy and mechanics of teaching is mentioned because of a need for good teachers. Occupational therapy teaching provides a unique professional opportunity for the person who really wants to teach, either academically or clinically. You must enjoy teaching, and if you teach well, your students will catch your enthusiasm at once. You do not merely throw out facts if you are teaching properly. You guide the students to active involvement in the learning process. You are influencing young minds, molding them into a firmer shape. This is one of the greatest satisfactions of teaching.

Teaching appointments in colleges or universities are usually of an academic nature with the rank of instructor, assistant professor, associate professor, or full professor. Clinical supervisors of field experience may hold academic appointments as adjunctive instructors if affiliated with a school program. Teaching ranks and titles vary with the different academic organization of colleges and universities. The descriptions in this chapter are limited primarily to entry-level academic and clinical teaching, but teaching experienced therapists in postprofessional master's degree programs also is possible for those who obtain the necessary experience and advanced education (see Chapter 6 for specific earnings in the field).

Academic teaching in a school usually includes the basic and social sciences applied to occupational therapy, plus instruction in therapeutic activities, while clinical teaching involves translating theory into practice by treating patients under the supervision of a registered therapist. Student field practice is arranged by the school faculty and includes a total of six to nine months of experience in the various clinical areas of occupational therapy under the auspices of approved affiliation centers.

A student performance evaluation report is kept on all occupational therapy students working in the field. This report is later discussed with the student by both the clinical supervisor and the supervisor of affiliation in the academic program.

Let us now turn our attention to the duties and responsibilities of two important positions in occupational therapy education that fall outside the realm of "pure" teaching: the school director and the fieldwork coordinator. Both play significant roles in educating today's therapists.

OCCUPATIONAL THERAPY PROGRAM DIRECTOR

The occupational therapy program director represents the facility to the administrators of the educational institution in which it is housed. The program may be at a university, college, or a technical school, as in the case of some occupational therapy assistant programs. The director must be a person who has accumulated wide knowledge of occupational therapy theory and practice. He or she must be an OTR and have attained at least a master's degree, and more appropriately a doctoral degree.

School administrators have many roles, but foremost among them is that of program developer. The tangible responsibilities are many and varied. Administrators may be asked to submit a floor plan for a new unit or select new equipment for the facility on short notice. They must work with the appropriate administrators in establishing a budget and then work within it. They must be familiar with business procedures such as setting up equitable pay scales and job descriptions and compiling forms for referrals and records for billing and inventory.

In addition to the proper academic credentials, the occupational therapy program director also must possess a personality suitable for coping with the myriad problems inherent in the position. He or she must have an even temperament and the ability to make decisions and must maintain a nonpartial relationship with faculty members and students. Working under extreme pressure is required at times, yet with all a dignified and controlled image must be maintained. In short, the director must be a leader.

The director is responsible for all departmental planning, the delegation of authority, and seeing that the work gets done. He or she attends upper-level departmental meetings and relays information back to the faculty. He or she conducts staff meetings where school problems relative to teaching programs, curriculum, disciplinary actions, and other pertinent affairs associated with student education are discussed.

The educational program director has to enforce all school and institutional rules. Conversely, there is an obligation to the staff to communicate their problems to the administration and to back them up in their requests to be heard. An open-door policy of free communication with staff and students must be maintained.

The director plans and assigns all of the teaching assignments and negotiates faculty contracts. The director also is responsible for student placement in clinical affiliations during the students' field practice, although the actual task may be delegated to faculty.

FIELDWORK COORDINATOR

The fieldwork coordinator of an educational program selects facilities for clinical education and assigns students to them for fieldwork experiences. He or she serves as the liaison between the educational program and the institution providing the clinical experience, monitoring progress, solving problems, and so forth. Institutions with larger staffs customarily have a clinician designated as the student supervisor. Evaluation forms are prepared for each student that reflect his or her performance in the clinical situation. The completed forms are sent to the fieldwork coordinators at individual students' schools.

CHAPTER 11

OTHER WORK AREAS

In this chapter we shall explore some related work areas where therapists can make significant contributions: clinical research, professional consulting, community health care, and in the public schools. All afford challenging and rewarding career opportunities for the enterprising therapist with special skills and goals.

CLINICAL RESEARCH

Active research is a part of the everyday professional life of the occupational therapist. It is this acquisition of knowledge through research, and the subsequent dissemination of knowledge through publication, that establishes the basic literature so necessary for the profession to grow in stature.

Research is not a "do-it-yourself" activity. One must train for the exacting science of systematic investigation, learning how to do research and joining forces with established investigators to compare results and procedures. Some techniques the prospective researcher must acquire are: how to construct a problem statement, how to form a hypothesis, how to set up a research design to prove or disprove the hypothesis, how to analyze data, how to use basic statistics, and how to present the results in a formal written report.

For those qualified and interested, occupational therapy offers an endless source of material for investigation. Researchers in occupational therapy are now concerning themselves with some of the following questions:

1. How do the results of developmental testing correlate with perceptual performance?
2. How do elderly patients or clients with dementia function on selected sensory integrative measures?
3. How would depressed psychotics react to organized leisure-type activities as compared to work activities?
4. How do sensorimotor integrative problems affect certain aspects of life functioning, including school performance?
5. What are the most effective therapy techniques for patients with specific neuromuscular problems?

Whether you participate actively in research efforts or simply keep up with new developments through reading the journals, clinical research will be important to you in your professional career.

CONSULTANT

A consultant is a person with considerable expertise on a particular subject or situation who is called in to offer suggestions on how to improve a situation or to comment on changes already made. The consultant does not provide continuing direct care but rather provides advice to the therapist or the facility requesting assistance.

It should be kept in mind that consultants do not have mandated authority. They do not order things to be changed. They advise, comment, and suggest. Usually the employing facility receives a written report upon completion of the consultancy. The suggestions may or may not be implemented.

Basic to successful consultation is the easy-mannered and self-controlled approach. Consultants listen a lot, do some investigating, and balance out the situation before offering advice. A great deal of tact and discretion is required in commenting and offering advice. The role of the consultant is characterized by the individual's specialized knowledge. The consultant is an outsider who tries to bring a clearer view of a situation.

Extended-care facilities and nursing homes, particularly since the Social Security Act of 1965 authorized Medicare, have increased the demand for consultants in this area. Most consultants have a minimum of five years of administrative clinical experience in a variety of situations, including some teaching and supervision.

Often a consultant is asked to assist in organizing a new department. This might include a myriad of tasks ranging from suggesting floor space and office allocations to devising record-keeping systems. In developing an initial program of treatment, consultants are frequently asked to coach the clinical staff in various procedures for handling patients.

Another type of consultant is the therapist with a basic knowledge of developmental learning materials. This type of consultancy usually takes place in educational workshops and seminars. Other consultants have expertise in sensorimotor treatment techniques, wheelchair positioning and adaptation, psychiatric treatment programming, work hardening programs, and additional areas too numerous to mention.

COMMUNITY HEALTH CARE

There is an increased public awareness of the benefits of total rehabilitation in connection with such disabling conditions as birth defects, arthritis, geriatric problems, amputations, and other chronic conditions that require long-term care. Close cooperation is required between the professional, public, and private agencies concerned with this total rehabilitation process.

The active involvement of occupational therapy professionals in community projects has been a growing trend in the last decade, and it continues to grow in importance in the field of social medicine and psychological services, as well as in preventive medicine.

Therapists are increasingly holding positions at the state level as consultants in home health-care programs. They participate in these programs as team members whose major concern is the maintenance of health and the prevention of disease and disability. Families have to be educated in the do's and don'ts of home care by means of public educational programs. In many instances, the health of patients has been restored to the point where adequate maintenance of their conditions can be sustained in the home setting, if adequate professional supervision is available.

Continuing health care services are provided by team members of a nursing staff and home-care aides. Their goal is to prevent further hospitalization or remissions. Occupational therapists, physical therapists, nurses, speech pathologists, nutritionists, and other specialists all contribute to such a program. Nutritional requirements are a very important issue in a home-care program, in order to ensure that the patient receives well-balanced meals specific to his or her condition.

Other community centers include drug and alcohol abuse facilities, set up especially for these conditions and sometimes housed in a rehabilitation center. Much preventive work is being done in these areas.

Interim and halfway houses for the recovering client who has had a mental illness are now quite numerous and provide a sheltering atmosphere of understanding and guidance until the client is ready to face, once again, the full reality of social living. These persons need supportive therapy for quite some time when recovering from the emotional and social problems that mental illness presents, in order to gain a sense of security before striking out on their own again.

There are also many large regional medical centers for long-term clients such as stroke, cancer, and heart patients, who need weekly check-ups and follow-up care. Occupational therapists are members of the health care teams that serve these clients at home and on an outpatient basis.

PUBLIC SCHOOLS

Laws mandating education and special services for all handicapped children have increased the need and demand for occupational therapy in the public school systems. Schools are at present the second largest employers of occupational therapists, after hospitals.

Occupational therapists have become specialists in areas dealing with limitations in skills and abilities related to learning. In addition to customary physical and psychosocial assessments, they regularly evaluate for problems in such areas as: visual tracking, convergence abilities, discrimination of figure-ground patterns, and reverse reading problems.

Occupational therapists in schools focus on abilities needed for learning activities. Movement and coordination needed for handwriting, perceptual skills important for reading, tolerance for sitting, and other abilities are all important. Occupational therapists counsel teachers and parents, recommending special equipment or activities that will help each child function at his or her best. In school settings, therapists participate in school meetings, help develop individual educational plans, and generally become a part of the educational system. Their hours and pay are generally comparable to those of teachers in the same setting.

Occupational therapists also can give teachers in-service training seminars within the school setting to help them learn how to position children, assist them in self-feeding, and adapt school equipment. Therapists also may be able to provide insight into neurologically based learning and attentional and behavioral disorders. Local school systems have in recent years added many ancillary services of this type to their programs. Counselors, psychologists, speech pathologists, physical therapists, and occupational therapists now have become integral parts of many public school programs.

The occupational therapist working in a community health program can become directly involved with other members of the health team, such as the public health nurse, in the detection of school-related problems. Occupational therapists in the schools are partners with other related services personnel, teachers, and administrators in the important task of providing the most appropriate environment and services for each child.

MISCELLANEOUS AREAS

As health insurance companies investigate necessary service coverage, they sometimes find a need for full-time therapists to provide advice. The same is true of employment agencies that place therapists. Some therapists start employment agencies for health professionals. Others, seeing the need for continuing education for health professionals, work full-time in setting up seminars and workshops.

Occupational therapists have developed businesses that establish contracts with hospitals and nursing homes to provide therapy services; they have become owners or employees of health product and therapy equipment companies; and they have become medical illustrators, writers, and editors. Indeed, their individual backgrounds and experience suit them for an astonishing variety of opportunities.

BIBLIOGRAPHY

PERIODICALS

AARC Times: The Magazine for the Respiratory Care Professional

American Association for Respiratory Care
   11030 Ables Lane
   Dallas, TX 75229-4593
   (972) 243-2272

American Journal of Occupational Therapy
Journal of Occupational Therapy Students
OT Practice

American Occupational Therapy Association
   4720 Montgomery Lane
   P.O. Box 31220
   Bethesda, MD 20824-1220
   (301) 652-2682

IMPACT (private practice)
Journal of Orthopaedic and Sports Play Therapy
Physical Therapy

American Physical Therapy Association
   1111 N. Fairfax Street
   Alexandria, VA 22314
   (703) 684-2782

Modalities

American Therapeutic Association
P.O. Box 612965
Dallas, TX 75261
(800) 357-1186

OCCUPATIONAL THERAPY BOOKS

American Occupational Therapy Association staff. *Managed Care: A Sourcebook for Occupational Therapy.* Bethesda, MD: American Occupational Therapy Association, Inc., 1996.

Anderson, Laura L. *Occupational Therapy as a Career: An Introduction to the Field and a Structured Method for Observation.* Philadelphia: F.A. Davis Co., 1998.

Brayley, Caroline R. *Clinician to Academician: A Handbook for Those Who Aspire to Become Faculty Members.* Bethesda, MD: American Occupational Therapy Association, Inc., 1996.

Hemphill, Barbara J. *Assessments in Occupational Therapy Mental Health: An Integrative Approach.* Thorofare, NJ: Slack Inc., 1999.

Hinojosa, Jim. *Frames of Reference for Pediatric Occupational Therapy.* Philadelphia: Lippincott-Williams & Wilkins, 1999.

Lewin, Jeanne E. *Creative Problem Solving in Occupational Therapy.* Philadelphia: Lippincott-Williams & Wilkins, 1998.

McEwen, Irene R. *Occupational & Physical Therapy in Educational Environments.* Binghampton, NY: The Haworth Press, Inc., 1995.

Newham, Paul. *The Healing Voice.* Boston: Element Books, Inc., 1999.

Reed, Kathlyn L. *Concepts of Occupational Therapy.* Philadelphia: Lippincott-Williams & Wilkins, 1999.

Ross, Mildred. *Adults with Developmental Disabilities: Current Approaches to Occupational Therapy.* Bethesda, MD: American Occupational Therapy Association, Inc., 1998.

Ryan S. *Making the Most of Fieldwork Education: A Practical Approach.* San Diego: Singular Publishing Group, Inc., 1996.

Wells, Shirley A. *Guide to Reasonable Accommodation for Practitioners with Disabilities: Fieldwork to Employment.* Bethesda, MD: American Occupational Therapy Association, Inc., 1998.

GENERAL JOB SEARCH BOOKS

Beatty, Richard H. *The Perfect Cover Letter.* New York: John Wiley & Sons, Inc., 1997.

Bolles, Richard N. *What Color Is Your Parachute?: A Practical Manual for Job-Hunters and Job-Changers.* Berkeley, CA: Ten Speed Press, 1996.

Dikel, Margaret Riley and Frances E. Roehm. *The Guide to Internet Job Searching.* Lincolnwood, IL: VGM Career Books, 2000.

Enelow, Wendy S. *Resume Winners from the Pros.* Manassas Park, VA: Impact Publications, 1998.

Kent, George. *Get Hired Today* (Here's How series). Lincolnwood, IL: VGM Career Books, 1999.

Noble, David F. *Gallery of Best Resumes for Two-Year Degree Graduates.* Indianapolis: JIST Works, Inc., 1996.

Troutman, Kathryn K. *The Federal Resume Guidebook.* Indianapolis: JIST Works, Inc., 1997.

VGM Career Books, eds. *Resumes for Health and Medical Careers.* Lincolnwood, IL: VGM Career Books, 1998.

Weddle, Peter D. *Internet Resumes.* Manassas, VA: Impact Publications, 1998.

Whitcomb, Susan Britton. *Resume Magic: Trade Secrets of a Professional Resume Writer.* Indianapolis: JIST Works, Inc., 1999.

Yate, Martin. *Knock 'Em Dead 1997.* Holbrook, MA: Adams Media Corporation, 1997.

PROFESSIONAL ASSOCIATIONS

American Association for Respiratory Care
  11030 Ables Lane
  Dallas, TX 75229-4593
  (972) 243-2272

American Occupational Therapy Association
  4720 Montgomery Lane
  P.O. Box 31220
  Bethesda, MD 20824-1220
  (301) 652-2682

American Physical Therapy Association
  1111 N. Fairfax Street
  Alexandria, VA 22314
  (703) 684-2782

American Therapeutic Association
  P.O. Box 612965
  Dallas, TX 75261
  (800) 357-1186

Association for Pediatric Therapists
  2784 Lantz Avenue
  San Jose, CA 95124
  (408) 377-9027

Association for Play Therapy
  2100 N. Winery Avenue
  Suite 104
  Fresno, CA 93703
  (559) 252-2278

Foundation for Physical Therapy
    1111 N. Fairfax Street
    Alexandria, VA 22314
    (703) 684-5984

National Association of Activity Professionals
    P.O. Box 23909
    Jackson, MS 39225
    (601) 853-3722

National Therapeutic Recreation Society
    22377 Belmont Ridge Road
    Ashburn, VA 20148
    (703) 858-0784

APPENDIX C

EDUCATIONAL PROGRAMS

The following occupational therapy and occupational therapy assistant programs are accredited by the Accreditation Council for Occupational Therapy Education of The American Occupational Therapy Association, Inc. Requests for specific information, should be directed to the admissions office or the occupational therapy program at each school. For more information check out the AOTA website at www.aota.com.

OCCUPATIONAL THERAPY PROGRAMS

Key

D   Developing programs that are accepting students and have applied for accreditation

1   Baccalaureate Degree

2   Postbaccalaureate Certificate

2A Certificate awarded to students in partial fulfillment of Master's degree

3   Professional (entry-level) Master's Degree

4   Combined Baccalaureate/Master's Degree

Alabama

D
Alabama State University
915 S. Jackson Street
Montgomery 36101

1
Tuskegee University
Basil O'Connor Hall
Tuskegee 36088

3
University of Alabama at Birmingham
102 Bishop Building, 900 S. 19th Street
Birmingham 35294

1
University of South Alabama
1504 Springhill Avenue, Room 5108
Mobile 36604

Arizona

3
Arizona School of Health Sciences
3210 W. Camelback Road
Phoenix 85017

D
Midwestern University
19555 N. 59th Avenue
Glendale 85308

Arkansas

1, 3
University of Central Arkansas
Box 5001
Conway 72035

California

1
California State University, Dominguez Hills
1000 E. Victoria Street
Carson 90747

1
Dominican College of San Rafael
50 Acacia Avenue
San Rafael 94901

1, 3, 4
Loma Linda University
School of Allied Health Professions
Nichol Hall, Room A903
Loma Linda 92350

3
Samuel Merritt College
370 Hawthorne Avenue
Oakland 94609

1, 3
San Jose State University
School of Applied Sciences and Arts
One Washington Square
San Jose 95192

D
Touro University of California
North Campus
San Francisco 94100

D
Touro University of California
South Campus
Los Angeles 90061

1, 3
University of Southern California
1540 Alcazar, CHP-133
Los Angeles 90033

Colorado

1, 3
Colorado State University
200 Occupational Therapy Building
Fort Collins 80523

Connecticut

1, 3
Quinnipiac College
School of Allied Health Sciences
275 Mount Carmel Avenue
Hamden 06518

D
Sacred Heart University
Fairfield 06432

1
University of Hartford
College of Education, Nursing, and Health Professions
200 Bloomfield Avenue
West Hartford 06117

District of Columbia

1
Howard University
Division of Allied Health Sciences
6th and Bryant Streets NW
Washington 20059

Florida

1
Barry University
11300 Northeast Second Avenue
Miami Shores 33161

1
Florida Agricultural and Mechanical University
223 Ware-Rhaney Building
Tallahassee 32307

D
Florida Gulf Coast University
10501 FGCU Building South
Fort Myers 33965

1, 2A
Florida International University
University Park Campus, CH 101
Miami 33199

3
Nova Southeastern University
Health Professions Division
3200 S. University Drive
Ft. Lauderdale 33328

1, 2A
University of Florida
Box 100164, HSC
Gainesville 32610–0164

3
University of St. Augustine for Health Sciences
Institute of Occupational Therapy
1 University Boulevard
St. Augustine 32086

Georgia

4
Brenau University
One Centennial Circle
Gainesville 30501

1
Medical College of Georgia
EF 102, Department of Occupational Therapy
Augusta 30912

Idaho

D
Idaho State University
Campus Box 8045
Pocatello 83209

Illinois

1
Chicago State University
College of Nursing and Allied Health Professions
9501 S. King Drive
Chicago 60628

3
Governor's State University
University Park 60466

3
Midwestern University
College of Health Sciences
555 31st Street
Downers Grove 60515

3
Rush University
Rush-Presbyterian-St. Luke's Medical Center
600 S. Paulina, Suite 1010
Chicago 60612

1,3
University of Illinois at Chicago
College of Health and Human Development Sciences
1919 W. Taylor Street, M/C 811
Chicago 60612

Indiana

1
Indiana University
School of Allied Health Sciences
1140 W. Michigan Street, Coleman Hall
Indianapolis 46202

3
University of Indianapolis
Graduate Programs in Occupational Therapy
1400 E. Hanna Avenue
Indianapolis 46227

1
University of Southern Indiana
8600 University Boulevard
Evansville 47710

Iowa

3
St. Ambrose University
518 W. Locust
Davenport 52803

Kansas

1
Newman University
3100 McCormick Avenue
Wichita 67213

1
University of Kansas Medical Center
School of Allied Health
3901 Rainbow Boulevard
Kansas City 66160

Kentucky

1, 2A
Eastern Kentucky University
Dizney 103
Richmond 40475

1
Spaulding University
851 S. Fourth Street
Louisville 40203

Louisiana

1
Louisiana State University Health Sciences Center
School of Allied Health Professions
1900 Gravier Street
New Orleans 70112

1
Louisiana State University Health Sciences Center
1501 Kings Highway
Shreveport 71130

1
Northeast Louisiana University
School of Allied Health Sciences
Monroe 71209

Maine

D
Husson College
One College Circle
Bangor 04401

3, 4
Lewiston-Auburn College
University of Southern Maine
51 Westminster Street
Lewiston 04240

4
University of New England
College of Arts and Sciences
Biddeford 04005

Maryland

1, 3
Towson State University
8000 York Road
Towson 21204

Massachusetts

American International College
1000 State Street, Box 46
Springfield 01109

D
Bay Path College
588 Longmeadow Street
Longmeadow 01106

1, 3
Boston University, Sargent College of Health and Rehabilitation Sciences
635 Commonwealth Avenue
Boston 02215

D
Salem State College
Salem 01970

3, 4
Springfield College
263 Alden Street
Springfield 01109

3
Tufts University-Boston School of Occupational Therapy
26 Winthrop Street
Medford 02155

1, 3
Worcester State College
486 Chandler Street
Worcester 01602

Michigan

1
Baker College of Flint
G-1050 W. Bristol Road
Flint 48507

1, 3
Eastern Michigan University
328 King Hall
Ypsilanti 48197

3
Grand Valley State University
322 Henry Hall, 1 Campus Drive
Allendale 49401

1
Saginaw Valley State University
7400 Bay Road
University Center 48710

1
Wayne State University
College of Pharmacy and Allied Health Professions
Detroit 48202

1, 3, 4
Western Michigan University
1201 Oliver Street
Kalamazoo 49008

Minnesota

1, 2, 3
College of St. Catherine
2004 Randolph Avenue
St. Paul 55105

3
University of Minnesota
Box 388, 426 Church Street SE
Minneapolis 55455

3, 4
College of St. Scholastica
1200 Kenwood Avenue
Duluth 55811

Mississippi

1
The University of Mississippi Medical Center
School of Health Related Professions
2500 North State Street
Jackson 39216

Missouri

1
Maryville University
13550 Conway Road
St. Louis 63141

3
Rockhurst College
College of Arts and Sciences
1100 Rockhurst Road
Kansas City 64110

1, D
Saint Louis University
School of Allied Health Professions
3437 Caroline Street
St. Louis 63104

1
University of Missouri-Columbia
School of Health Related Professions
407 Lewis Hall
Columbia 65211

3
Washington University School of Medicine
4444 Forest Park Avenue
St. Louis, MO 63110

Nebraska

1
College of Saint Mary
1901 S. 72nd Street
Omaha 68124

1
Creighton University
School of Pharmacy and Allied Health
2500 California Plaza
Omaha 68178

New Hampshire

1, 2
University of New Hampshire
School of Health and Human Services
Hewitt Hall, 4 Library Way
Durham 03824

New Jersey

1, 3
Kean University
Townsend T209, P.O. Box 411
Union 07083

D
Richard Stockton College of New Jersey
Jim Leeds Road
Pomona 08240

3
Seton Hall University
400 S. Orange Avenue
South Orange 07079

New Mexico

1
The University of New Mexico
School of Medicine
Health Science and Services Building
Room 215
Albuquerque 87131

New York

3
Columbia University
710 West 168th Street
New York 10032

1, 4
Dominican College
470 Western Highway
Orangeburg 10962

4
D'Youville College
320 Porter Avenue
Buffalo 14201–1084

4
Ithaca College
200 Smiddy Hall
Ithaca 14850

1
Keuka College
Keuka Park 14478

D
Long Island University, Brooklyn Campus
University Plaza
Brooklyn 11201

4
Mercy College
555 Broadway
Dobbs Ferry 10522

1
New York Institute of Technology
P.O. Box 8000
Old Westbury 11568

1, 3
New York University
School of Education
35 W. 4th Street, 11th Floor
New York 10012

4
Sage Colleges
45 Ferry Street
Troy 12180

1
State University of New York at Stony Brook
School of Health Technology and Management
L2-031
Stony Brook 11794

1
State University of New York Health Science Center at Brooklyn
450 Clarkson Avenue, Box 81
Brooklyn 11203

4
Touro College
1700 Union Boulevard
Dix Hills, NY 11746

1
University at Buffalo, State University of New York
515 Stockton Kimball Tower
3435 Main Street
Buffalo 14214

1
Utica College of Syracuse University
Division of Health Sciences
1600 Burrstone Road
Utica 13502

1
York College of the City University of New York
94–20 Guy R. Brewer Boulevard
Jamaica 11451

North Carolina

1
East Carolina University
School of Allied Health Sciences
Greenville 27858

1
Lenoir-Rhyne College
Box 7547
Hickory 28603

3
University of North Carolina at Chapel Hill
Medical School, Wing E, CB #7120
Chapel Hill 27599

D
Winston-Salem State University
P.O. Box 19368
601 Martin Luther King Jr. Drive
Winston-Salem 27110

North Dakota

1, 3
University of Mary
7500 University Drive
Bismarck 58504

1
University of North Dakota
Box 7126, University Station
Grand Forks 58202

Ohio

1, 2
Cleveland State University
2501 Euclid Avenue
Cleveland 44115

3
Medical College of Ohio at Toledo
School of Allied Health
3015 Arlington Avenue
Toledo 43699

1, 2
Ohio State University
School of Allied Medical Professions
1583 Perry Street
Columbus 43210

1
Shawnee State University
940 Second Street
Portsmouth 45662

1, 4
University of Findlay
1000 N. Main Street
Findlay 45840

1, 2
Xavier University
3800 Victory Parkway
Cincinnati 45207–7341

Oklahoma

1, 3
University of Oklahoma Health Sciences Center
College of Allied Health
801 NE 13th Street
Oklahoma City 73190

Oregon

3
Pacific University
2043 College Way
Forest Grove 97116

Pennsylvania

1
Alvernia College
400 Saint Bernardine Street
Reading 19607

3
Chatham College
Woodland Road
Pittsburgh 15232

3, 4
College Misericordia
Division of Health Sciences
301 Lake Street
Dallas 18612

3, 4
Duquesne University
John G. Rangos School of Health Sciences
Room 234
Pittsburgh 15282

1
Elizabethtown College
One Alpha Drive
Elizabethtown 17022

4
Gannon University
University Station
Erie 16541

1
Mount Aloysius College
7373 Admiral Peary Highway
Cresson 16630

1
Pennsylvania State University
Campus Drive
Mont Alto 17237

D
Philadelphia University
School House Lane & Henry Avenue
Philadelphia 19144

D
Saint Francis College
P.O. Box 600
Loretto 15940

1, 2A
Temple University
College of Allied Health Professions
3307 North Broad Street
Philadelphia 19140

1, 3
Thomas Jefferson University
College of Health Professions
130 S. 9th Street
Philadelphia 19107

1
University of Pittsburgh
School of Health and Rehabilitation Sciences
5022 Forbes Tower
Pittsburgh 15260

4
University of the Sciences in Philadelphia
600 S. 43rd Street, Box 24
Philadelphia 19104

1
University of Scranton
Scranton 18510

Puerto Rico

1
University of Puerto Rico
Medical Sciences Campus
P.O. Box 365067
San Juan 00936

South Carolina

1, 3
Medical University of South Carolina
College of Health Professions
171 Ashley Avenue, Room 125-CHP
Charleston 29425

South Dakota

3
University of South Dakota
414 E. Clark Street
Vermillion 57069

Tennessee

3, 4
Belmont University
1900 Belmont Boulevard
Nashville 37212

D
Milligan College
P.O. Box 130
Milligan College 37682

1
Tennessee State University
School of Allied Health Professions
3500 John Merritt Boulevard
Nashville 37209

D
University of Tennessee–Chattanooga
615 McCallie Avenue
Chattanooga 37403

1
University of Tennessee–Memphis
822 Beale Street
Memphis, TN 38163

Texas

1
Texas Tech University Health Sciences Center
School of Allied Health
3601 4th Street
Lubbock 79430

1, 2, 3
Texas Woman's University
Box 425648, TWU Station
Denton, TX 76204-1718

1
University of Texas at El Paso
Occupational Therapy Program
1101 N. Campbell Street
El Paso 79902

1, 3
The University of Texas Health Science Center at San Antonio
7703 Floyd Curl Drive
San Antonio 78284

D
University of Texas Pan-American
1201 W. University Drive
Edinburg 78539

1
University of Texas School of Allied Health Sciences at Galveston
The University of Texas Medical Branch at Galveston, J–28
301 University Boulevard
Galveston 77555

Utah

D
University of Utah
520 Wakara Way
Salt Lake City 84108

Virginia

1
College of Health Sciences
Community Hospital of Roanoke Valley
920 S. Jefferson Street
Roanoke 24016

D
James Madison University
College of Integrated Science and Technology, MSC 4007
Harrisonburg 22807

3, 4
Shenandoah University
333 W. Cork Street
Winchester 22601

1, 3
Virginia Commonwealth University
P.O. Box 980008
Richmond 23298

Washington

D
Eastern Washington University
526 5th Street, Room 106
Cheney 90004

1, 3
The University of Puget Sound
1500 N. Warner
Tacoma 98416

3
University of Washington
Box 356490
Seattle 98195

West Virginia

3
West Virginia University
Robert C. Byrd Health Sciences Center
P.O. Box 9139-HSN
Morgantown 26506

Wisconsin

1, 3
Concordia University Wisconsin
12800 N. Lake Shore Drive
Mequon 53092

1
Mount Mary College
2900 N. Menomonee River Parkway
Milwaukee 53222

D
University of Wisconsin–La Crosse
1725 State Street
La Crosse 54601

1
University of Wisconsin–Madison
1300 University Avenue (2110/MSC)
Madison 53706

1, 4
The University of Wisconsin–Milwaukee
School of Allied Health Professions
P.O. Box 413
Milwaukee 53201

Wyoming

1
University of North Dakota at Casper College
125 College Drive
Casper 82601

OCCUPATIONAL THERAPY ASSISTANT PROGRAMS

Key

D   Developing programs that are accepting students and have applied for accreditation
1   Associate Degree
2   Certificate Program

Alabama

1
Jefferson State Community College
Pinson Valley Parkway
2601 Carson Road
Birmingham 35215

1
Wallace State Community College
P.O. Box 2000
Hanceville 35077

Arizona

1
Apollo College
2701 W. Bethany Home Road
Phoenix 85017

Arkansas

D
South Arkansas Community College
300 S. West Avenue
El Dorado 71731

California

1
Andon College at Modesto
1700 McHenry Village Way
Modesto 95350

1
Grossmont College
8800 Grossmont College Drive
El Cajon 92020

1
Loma Linda University
SAHP-Nichol Hall, Room A912
Loma Linda 92350

1
Maric College of Medical Careers
3666 Kearny Villa Road
San Diego 92123

1, 2
Mount St. Mary's College
Doheny Campus
10 Chester Place
Los Angeles 90007

1
Sacramento City College
Allied Health Department
3835 Freeport Boulevard
Sacramento 95822

1
Santa Ana College
1530 W. 17th Street
Santa Ana 92706

1
Western Career College
170 Bayfair Mall
San Leandro 94578

1
Western Institute of Science and Health
130 Avram Avenue
Rohnert Park 94928

Colorado

1
Arapahoe Community College
2500 W. College Drive
Littleton 80160

1
Denver Technological College
925 S. Niagara Street
Denver 80224

1
Morgan Community College
17800 Road 20
Fort Morgan 80701

1
Pueblo Community College
900 W. Orman Avenue
Pueblo 81004

1
Westwood College of Technology
7350 N. Broadway
Denver 80221

Connecticut

1
Briarwood College
2279 Mount Vernon Road
Southington 06489

D
Housatonic Community–Technical College
900 Lafayette Boulevard
Bridgeport 06604

1
Manchester Community–Technical College
P. O. Box 1046
60 Bidwell Street, MS # 29
Manchester 06040

Delaware

1
Delaware Technical and Community College
P.O. Box 610
Georgetown 19947

1
Delaware Technical and Community College
333 Shipley Street
Wilmington 19801

Florida

1
Central Florida Community College
P.O. Box 1388
Ocala 34478

D
Chipola Junior College
3094 Indian Circle
Marianna 32446

1
Daytona Beach Community College
1200 International Speedway Boulevard
Daytona Beach 32120

D
Florida Hospital College of Health Sciences
800 Lake Estelle Drive
Orlando 32803

1
Hillsborough Community College
P.O. Box 30030
Tampa 33630

1
Keiser College
1500 NW 49th Street
Ft. Lauderdale 33309

D
Keiser College
900 S. Babcock Street
Melbourne 32901

1
Manatee Community College
5840 26th Street West
P.O. Box 1849
Bradenton 34207

1
Palm Beach Community College
4200 S. Congress Avenue
Lake Worth 33461

D
Polk Community College
Math, Science, and Health Division
999 Avenue H, Northeast
Winter Haven 33881

Georgia

D
Augusta Technical Institute
3116 Deans Bridge Road
Augusta 30906

1
Darton College
2400 Gillionville Road
Albany 31707

1
Middle Georgia College
1100 Second Street SE
Cochran 31014

1
Northwestern Technical Institute
265 Bicentennial Trail
Rock Spring 30739

1
Thomas Technical Institute
15689 U.S. Highway 19 North
Thomasville 31792

Hawaii

1
University of Hawaii/Kapiolani Community College
Health Sciences Department
4303 Diamond Head Road
Honolulu 96816

Idaho

1
American Institute of Health Technology, Inc.
6600 Emerald
Boise 83704

Illinois

1
Black Hawk College
6600 34th Avenue
Moline 61265

1
College of DuPage
Occupational and Vocational Education
425 22nd Street
Glen Ellyn 60137

1
Illinois Central College
201 SW Adams
East Peoria 61635

1
Lincoln Land Community College
5250 Shepherd Road
Springfield 62794

1
Parkland College
2400 W. Bradley Avenue
Champaign 61821

1
South Suburban College of Cook County
15800 S. State Street
South Holland 60473

1
Southern Illinois Collegiate Common Market
3213 S. Park Avenue
Herrin 62948

1
Wright College
4300 N. Narragansett Avenue
Chicago 60634

Indiana

1
Ivy Tech State College–Central Indiana
One W. 26th Street
Indianapolis 46208

1
Michiana College
1030 E. Jefferson Boulevard
South Bend 46617

D
Professional Careers Institute
7302 Woodland Drive
Indianapolis 46278

D
University of Saint Francis
2701 Spring Street
Fort Wayne 46808

1
University of Southern Indiana
8600 University Boulevard
Evansville 47712

Iowa

1
Kirkwood Community College
P.O. Box 2068
6301 Kirkwood Boulevard SW
Cedar Rapids, IA 52406

1
Western Iowa Tech Community College
4647 Stone Avenue
Sioux City 51102

Kansas

1
Barton County Community College
245 NE 30th Road
Great Bend 67530

1
Kansas City Kansas Community College
P.O. Box 12951
7250 State Avenue
Kansas City 66112

Kentucky

1
Jefferson Community College
Downtown Campus
109 E. Broadway
Louisville 40202

2
Madisonville Technical College
750 N. Laffoon Street
Madisonville 42431

Louisiana

1
Delgado Community College
City Park Campus
615 City Park Avenue
New Orleans 70119

1
Northeast Louisiana University
School of Allied Health Sciences
College of Pharmacy and Health Sciences
Monroe 71209

Maine

1
Kennebec Valley Technical College
Western Avenue
P.O. Box 29
Fairfield 04937

Maryland

1
Allegany College of Medicine
12401 Willowbrook Road SE
Cumberland 21502

1
Community College of Baltimore County at Catonsville
800 S. Rolling Road
Catonsville 21228

Massachusetts

1
Bay Path College
588 Longmeadow Street
Longmeadow 01106

1
Bay State College
31 St. James Avenue
Boston 02116

1
Becker College
61 Sever Street, Box 15071
Worcester MA 01615

1
Bristol Community College
Fall River 02720

1
Greenfield Community College
270 Main Street
Greenfield 01301

1
Lasell College
1844 Commonwealth Avenue
Auburndale 02466

1
Massachusetts Bay Community College
50 Oakland Street
Wellesley Hills 02481

1
Mount Ida College
Junior College Division
777 Dedham Street
Newton Centre 02159

1
North Shore Community College
1 Ferncroft Road
Danvers 01923

1
Quinsigamond Community College
670 W. Boylston Street
Worchester 01606

1
Springfield Technical Community College
One Armory Square
Springfield 01105

Michigan

1
Baker College of Muskegon
1903 Marquette Avenue
Muskegon 49442

1
Charles Stewart Mott Community College
Southern Lakes Branch Campus
2100 W. Thompson Road
Fenton 48430

1
Davenport College, Kalamazoo Campus
4123 W. Main Street
Kalamazoo 49006

1
Grand Rapids Community College
143 Bostwick, NE
Grand Rapids 49503

1, D
Lake Michigan College
Bertrand Crossing
1905 Foundation Drive
Niles 49120

1
Macomb Community College
44575 Garfield Road
Clinton Township 48038

1
Schoolcraft College
1751 Radcliff Street
Garden City 48135

1
Wayne County Community College
1001 W. Fort Street
Detroit, MI 48226

Minnesota

1
Anoka-Hennepin Technical College
1355 W. Highway 10
Anoka 55303

1
College of St. Catherine–Minneapolis
601 25th Avenue South
Minneapolis 55454

1
Lake Superior College
2101 Trinity Road
Duluth 55811

1
Northwest Technical College
Highway 220 North
East Grand Forks 56721

1
Riverland Community College
1900 8th Avenue NW
Austin 55912

Mississippi

D
Holmes Community College
412 W. Ridgeland Avenue
Ridgeland 39157

1
Pearl River Community College
5448 U.S. Highway 49 South
Hattiesburg 39401

Missouri

1
Missouri College
10073 Manchester Road
St. Louis 63122

1
Penn Valley Community College
3201 Southwest Trafficway
Kansas City 64111

D
St. Charles County Community College
4601 Mid Rivers Mall Drive
St. Peters 63376

1
St. Louis Community College at Meramec
11333 Big Bend Boulevard
St. Louis 63122

1
Sanford-Brown College
Hazelwood Campus
75 Village Square
Hazelwood 63042

Montana

1
Montana State University, College of Technology
Allied Health Department
P.O. Box 6010
Great Falls 59405

Nebraska

1
Clarkson College
101 S. 42nd Street
Omaha 68131

Nevada

1
Community College of Southern Nevada
6375 W. Charleston Boulevard-900
Las Vegas 89146

New Hampshire

1
Hesser College
Occupational Therapy Assistant Program
3 Sundial Avenue
Manchester 03103

1
New Hampshire Community Technical College-Claremont
One College Drive
Claremont, NH 03743–9707

New Jersey

1
Atlantic Cape Community College
Allied Health Department
5100 Black Horse Pike
Mays Landing 08330

1
Union County College
232 E. Second Street
Plainfield 07060

New Mexico

1
Eastern New Mexico University
Division of Health
52 University Boulevard
Roswell 88202

1
Western New Mexico University
P.O. Box 680
Silver City 88062

New York

D
Adirondack Community College
640 Bay Road
Queensbury 12804

1
Erie Community College
North Campus
6205 Main Street
Williamsville 14221

1
Genesee Community College
One College Road
Batavia 14020

1
Herkimer County Community College
Reservoir Road
Herkimer 13350

1
Jamestown Community College
525 Falconer Street
Jamestown 14701

1
LaGuardia Community College
31-10 Thomson Avenue
Long Island City 11101

1
Maria College
700 New Scotland Avenue
Albany 12208

1
Mercy College
355 Broadway
Dobbs Ferry 10522

1
Orange County Community College
115 S. Street
Middletown 10940

1
Rockland Community College
145 College Road
Suffern 10901

D
State University of New York at Canton
Cornell Drive
Canton 13617

1
Suffolk County Community College
Crooked Hill Road
Brentwood 11717

1
Touro College
School of Health Sciences
27-33 W. 23rd Street
New York 10010

North Carolina

1
Caldwell Community College and Technical Institute
2855 Hickory Boulevard
Hudson 28638

1
Cape Fear Community College
1637 Lawson Street
Durham 27703

1
Durham Technical Community College
1637 Lawson Street
Durham 27703

1
Pitt Community College
Highway 11, South
P.O. Drawer 7007
Greenville 27835

1
Rockingham Community College
P.O. Box 38
Wentworth 27375

1
Southwestern Community College
Sylva 28779

1
Stanly Community College
Albemarle 28001

North Dakota

1
North Dakota State College of Science
Mayme Green Allied Health Facility
Wahpeton 58076

Ohio

1
Cincinnati State Technical and Community College
3520 Central Parkway
Cincinnati 45223

1
Cuyahoga Community College
2900 Community College Avenue
Cleveland 44115

1
Kent State University
East Liverpool Campus
400 E. Fourth Street
East Liverpool 43920

1
Lima Technical College
4240 Campus Drive
Lima 45804

1
Lourdes College
6832 Convent Boulevard
Sylvania 43560

1
Muskingum Area Technical College
1555 Newark Road
Zanesville 43701

1
Owens Community College
Toledo Campus, Oregon Road
P.O. Box 10000
Toledo 43699

1
Shawnee State University
940 Second Street
Portsmouth 45662

1
Sinclair Community College
444 W. Third Street
Dayton 45402

1
Stark State College of Technology
6200 Frank Avenue NW
Canton, OH 44720

Oklahoma

1
Caddo-Kiowa Vocational Technical Center/Southwestern
    Oklahoma State University
P.O. Box 190
Fort Cobb 73038

1
Oklahoma City Community College
Health, Social Sciences, and Human Services Division
7777 S. May Avenue
Oklahoma City 73159

1
Tulsa Community College, Metro Campus
Allied Health Services Division
909 S. Boston Avenue
Tulsa 74119

Oregon

1
Mt. Hood Community College
26000 SE Stark Street
Gresham 97030

Pennsylvania

1
Clarion University of Pennsylvania
1801 W. First Street
Oil City 16301

1
Community College of Allegheny County/Boyce Campus
595 Beatty Road
Monroeville 15146

1
Harcum College
750 Montgomery Avenue
Bryn Mawr, PA 19010

1
ICM School of Business and Medical Careers
10 Wood Street at Fort Pitt Boulevard
Pittsburgh 15222

1
Lehigh Carbon Community College
4525 Education Park Drive
Schnecksville 18078

1
Mount Aloysius College
7373 Admiral Peary Highway
Cresson 16630

1
Pennsylvania College of Technology
One College Avenue
Williamsport 17701

1
Pennsylvania State University
Mont Alto Campus, Campus Drive
Mont Alto 17237

Puerto Rico

1
Humacao University College
University of Puerto Rico
CUH Postal Station
Humacao 00791

Rhode Island

1
Community College of Rhode Island
Satellite Campus at Newport Hospital
275 Broadway
Newport 02840

1
New England Institute of Technology
2500 Post Road
Warwick 02886

South Carolina

1
Greenville Technical College
506 S. Pleasantburg Drive
P.O. Box 5616
Greenville 29606

1
Trident Technical College
P.O. Box 118067
Charleston 29411

South Dakota

1
Lake Area Technical Institute
230 11th Street
Watertown 57201

1
National American University
321 Kansas Street
Rapid City 57709

Tennessee

D
Knoxville Business College
1637 Downtown W. Boulevard
Knoxville 37919

1
Nashville State Technical Institute
120 White Bridge Road
P.O. Box 90285
Nashville 37209

1
Roane State Community College
276 Patton Lane
Harriman 37748

Texas

2
Academy of Health Sciences, U.S. Army
Army Medical Specialists Corps Division
3151 Scott Road, Suite 1230
Fort Sam Houston 78234
(limited to enlisted personnel in Army and Air Force)

1
Amarillo College
Amarillo 79178

1
Austin Community College
1020 Grove Boulevard
Austin 78736

1
Del Mar College
Department of Allied Health
101 Baldwin & Ayers
Corpus Christi 78404

2
Houston Community College
Health Careers Division
3100 Shenandoah
Houston 77021

D
Kingwood College, North Harris Montgomery Community College District
20000 Kingwood Drive
Kingwood 77339

1
Laredo Community College
West End Washington Street
Laredo 78040

1
Navarro College
3200 W. 7th Avenue
Corsicana 75110

1
North Central Texas College
601 E. Hickory Street, Suite B
Denton 76201

1
Panola College
1109 W. Panola
Carthage 75633

1
St. Philip's College
1801 Martin Luther King Street
San Antonio 78203

1
San Jacinto College South
13735 Beamer Road
Houston 77089

1
South Texas Community College
P.O. Box 9701
McAllen 78502

D
Texas Navarro College at Eastfield College
3737 Motley Drive at I-30
Mesquite 75150

1
Tomball College
30555 Tomball Parkway
Tomball 77375

Utah

1
Salt Lake Community College
P.O. Box 30808
Salt Lake City 84130

Vermont

1
Champlain College
163 S. Willard Street
Burlington 05402

Virginia

1
College of Health Sciences
Community Hospital of Roanoke Valley
920 S. Jefferson Street
Roanoke 24031

1
J. Sargeant Reynolds Community College
P.O. Box 85622
Richmond 23285

2
Southwest Virginia Community College
P.O. Box SVCC
Richlands 24641

2
Tidewater Community College
1700 College Crescent
Virginia Beach 23456

Washington

1
Green River Community College
12401 SE 320th Street
Auburn 98002

1
Yakima Valley Community College
Sixteenth Avenue and Nob Hill Boulevard
P.O. Box 22520
Yakima 98907

West Virginia

1
The College of West Virginia
School of Health Sciences
P.O. Box AG
Beckley 25802

Wisconsin

1
Fox Valley Technical College
1825 N. Bluemound Drive
Appleton 54913

1
Madison Area Technical College
211 N. Carroll Street
Madison 53703

1
Milwaukee Area Technical College
700 W. State Street
Milwaukee 53233

1
Western Wisconsin Technical College
304 Sixth Street N.
P.O. Box C-908
LaCrosse 54602

1
Wisconsin Indianhead Technical College–Ashland Campus
2100 Beaser Avenue
Ashland 54806

Wyoming

1
Casper College
125 College Drive
Casper 82601